RESPONDING TO THE

CHALLENGE

of

EVOLUTION

RESPONDING TO THE

CHALLENGE *of* EVOLUTION

KEVIN LOGAN

Victor®

The Bible Teacher's Teacher

COOK COMMUNICATIONS MINISTRIES
Colorado Springs, Colorado • Paris, Ontario
KINGSWAY COMMUNICATIONS LTD
Eastbourne, England

Victor® is an imprint of
Cook Communications Ministries, Colorado Springs, CO 80918
Cook Communications, Paris, Ontario
Kingsway Communications, Eastbourne, England

RESPONDING TO THE CHALLENGE OF EVOLUTION

First published 2002.
North American edition 2005

The Web site addresses recommended throughout this book are offered as a
resource to you. These Web sites are not intended in any way to be or imply an
endorsement on the part of Cook Communications Ministries, nor do we vouch
for their content.

Library of Congress Cataloging-in-Publication Data

Logan, Kevin, 1943-
  Responding to the challenge of evolution / Kevin Loga.
    p. cm.
  Includes index.
  ISBN 0-7814-4184-6 (pbk.)
  1. Creationism. 2. Bible and evolution. 3. Evolution (Biology)--Religious
aspects--Christianity. I. Title.
  BS651.L64 2005
  231.7'652--dc22
                                    2004026761

Originally published by
KINGSWAY COMMUNICATIONS LTD
Lottbridge Drove, Eastbourne BN23 6NT, England.

To Linda,
my long-suffering better half.
Also Peter, Ruth, and Lois;
and Cathryn and Simon.

Contents

THANKS

My name is on the cover, but many others should be there also. I am indebted to all who helped with my research, and the main ones are noted as we go through the book.

My critical readers assisted in brutally honest ways, as requested. My deepest thanks to Andrew Barton; Paul Bold; Enid Briggs (who is also my Reader and who did much in the parish during the six weeks of writing); Geoff Chapman; David Graham; Cathryn, Linda, and Peter Logan; Vera Richmond; and Robin Wilding.

Thank you to my parish of Christ Church, Accrington, and its Parochial Church Council and church members, who allowed me time to write. They were willing to put their own church and pastoral needs on hold, and I am grateful.

As always, Kingsway Publications gave me great encouragement and help, especially Richard Herkes and Carolyn Owen.

My support team included Enid Briggs, Betty Clegg, Adele and Stephen Cox, Harry and Nora Davies, David and Barbara Graham, and Emily Storey.

None of the above should be held accountable for the views in the book.

—Kevin Logan

❖ INTRODUCTION

Chapter 1

Battle Lines Are Drawn

I s the Prime Minister happy to allow the teaching of creation-ism alongside Darwin's theory of evolution in state schools?"

It was one of the shortest Prime Minister Question Time questions on record in Britain, yet, together with the Prime Minister's answer, it generated one of the biggest furies in the media. The ripples are still stirring science, religion, and education.

"First," smiled Tony Blair, "I am very happy. Secondly, I know that the Honorable Lady [Dr. Jenny Tonge, Member of Parliament for Richmond Park] is referring to a school in the Northeast, and I think that certain reports about what it has been teaching are somewhat exaggerated."[1]

It was what the Prime Minister said next that created the flood of headlines, television sound bites, and both scientific and religious consternation. "It would be very unfortunate if concerns about the issue were seen to remove the very strong incentive to ensure that we get as diverse a school system as we properly can."

In one sentence, the leader of Britain appeared to elevate creationism to the Everest of evolution, and the howls of disbelief from the scientific and religious Sherpas, who had carried it to its heady supremacy, could suddenly be heard.

"Ludicrous!" cried Richard Dawkins, the Charles Simonyi Professor of the Public Understanding of Science at Oxford. "Young-earth creationists teach bad science and worse religion."

Bishops, fearing a backlash against in-vogue faith schools, joined in the growing criticisms of Emmanuel City Technology College in Gateshead as it pondered whether to include creationism teaching. Sixteen scientists and clerics wrote to the Prime Minister, "We believe that curricula in such schools should be strictly monitored in order that the respective disciplines of science and religious studies are properly respected."

Steve Jones, Professor of Genetics at University College, London, accused the "creationists who have hijacked state-funded English schools" of spreading "pure poison."[2] Tongue-in-cheek, he explained:

> I have for many years, albeit without formal training, had a deep interest in designing a large passenger aircraft. Because of blind prejudice of the aviation establishment, none has yet been built. ... I know, as a biologist,

that feathers are the way forward, and if provided with enough cash by a rich bird-fancier,
I would be happy to educate a new generation
of engineers to believe in my own ideas—or,
in all fairness, to afford them the same weight
as the now controversial Boeing Theory.

This implication that creationists are enthusiasts with no training is rather impish considering many of them are at least as qualified as Professor Jones, and with similar titles. However, it appears to be true that creationists are thinner on the ground when it comes to biology.

Understandably, this is the normal temperature in the hot air that envelops what is becoming a fierce controversy in normally laid-back Britain. Criticism from the other side is just as potent.

"I worry about Professor Dawkins, and his crackpot theory that the universe evolved from some kind of accidental explosion at the dawn of time," pens *Daily Telegraph* columnist Tom Utley. "It's not that I'm against far-fetched theories in general. Who knows, the professor might be right—although it seems much more plausible that all life and matter were created by a supreme and intelligent deity, as most of the cleverest men have believed for many thousands of years. It may even be that we're both right."

Mr. Utley then explained that what really worried him was "the superstitious way in which Professor Dawkins clings to his theory, and refuses to admit even the slightest possibility that anybody else might be right. There is something almost hysterical about his attack on science teachers at Emmanuel College."[3]

In the midst of all this mayhem, a quiet, bespectacled Emmanuel head, Nigel McQuoid, sat in his study. Asked by a gently probing David Frost to explain creation over thousands of years as opposed to evolution over billions of years, Mr. McQuoid replied,

> The national curriculum in science actually asks us to look at the whole controversy around the theory of evolution, and that whole question begs the idea that people look at this evidence in different ways. For many years, people have looked at the evidence and said we can't actually age the earth. Some scientific papers, recently, have begun to question these things. And, in college, we have decided that we must look at these scientific papers before we present them to the children, to see whether or not they have any scientific validity. That's a debate, and I suppose we're concerned that people are trying to stop that debate, because we feel that science has been best when it's allowed itself to ask these difficult questions. And when science says we've got everything sorted—we've got everything sussed—I think that's a very dangerous position.

David Frost pushed him further: "And where do you stand on this issue yourself?"

The head replied, "I believe that God made the world. I don't know how He did it.... I don't know how long it took

Him. ... I think we're going to teach children that they must look at all sides and ask good questions."

ON A PERSONAL NOTE

Mr. McQuoid's last sentence, it seems to me, is not only true for the children of Gateshead but for people of all ages everywhere. We must look at both sides, and that is the aim of this book.

I will be the reporter of facts, theories, and expert opinion. You are invited to be the jury. My qualification for this task, besides a long interest in the subject, is my training as a journalist and copyeditor—gathering the facts; reporting the news and views; telling it as it is, and as it happens. The good print journalist—the old-fashioned sort, skilled at providing the truth rather than the story-at-any-cost—answers the when, where, what, why, and how and then leaves the rest to the reader.

This is doubly important in this multidisciplinary area. The biologist is not much better than the average layman when it comes to geology. The master of geology may be the learner cosmologist. No one in the disciplines mentioned so far would assist the linguist, paleontologist, theologian, or physicist (classical or quantum). And, of course, there are even knowledge gaps within disciplines. The average biologist would be struggling in the minute niceties of molecular biology. To have a complete understanding of our issue, one would also need degrees in genetics, sociology, psychology, and half the other -ologies. Such is the breadth of what we dare to examine.

This makes it all the more alarming that almost every one of the hundreds of books, CDs, pamphlets, tapes, videos, and Web sites I've ever digested on evolution and creation over twenty-five years has been produced from a "believer's" stance. I often feel bombarded by evangelists browbeating me with their assorted Bibles, and they constantly appear guilty of overstating their arguments while exaggerating the faults of the opposition.

Wouldn't it be a change, I mused, to read a book that presented the facts, left out the vitriol, and allowed the reader to come to his or her own conclusion? I offer this as such. I learned this method in the hard grind of factual, daily newspaper journalism, in an era when getting the facts wrong was a reason to get fired fast. In later life, I was ordained into the ministry and continued a different form of journalism through seven nonfiction books, one novel, a host of columns and contributions in newspapers, and twenty-seven years of reporting the good news of Christianity as a Church of England minister.[4]

However, even facts can be slanted by editorial bias, so you need a quick brief on where I stand. I was happy with evolution throughout my education, journalism, and first years as a Christian (I was a late starter after conversion at twenty-eight). If God wanted to create that way, then that was fine by me. I then spent twenty-five years as a creationist, for three reasons:

1. Media "pop" scientists started to use evolution to eliminate God, or they televised nature as if it were the only thing to be worshiped.

2. As irritation grew, the old reporter instincts became unhappy with too many unanswered questions. These we will meet later.

3. Finally and pragmatically, God's Word worked successfully in everyday life and relations. Then, serious study for the ministry brought a choice: do I treat it—and Genesis in particular—as myth or as literal and historical? I concluded, in my wisdom or otherwise, that I needed far more answers before moving from the literal. I was not prepared to swap a working certainty in my daily life for a questionable theory.

And now? Well, I have moved—even more so as I researched for what you now read. In fact, I could write a book about it. Come with me and see what I found.

My motive is, I hope, similar to yours. I want to know what can be known about perhaps the most difficult subject that has faced us in the last 150 years, ever since Charles Darwin published *On the Origin of Species*. I also want to recognize what is speculation, hearsay, or unsupported fundamentalist propaganda coming from both sides of the debate.

Above all, I want to know all this as leader of a chaplaincy team in a church secondary school. What do I tell the hundreds I face each week? The last thing any of us wish to do is to pass on ignorance or any belief or theory that might hinder or harm young people in their social, moral, or spiritual development.

So, here is the issue: the facts, the fables, the theories, the experts.

THE TECHNICAL BITS

I have tried hard to stay within normal, everyday language. From time to time, even this will be mind-boggling. We are, after all, dealing with most aspects of science, and sometimes at a deep level. At the slightest sign of a "boggle," do please feel free to skip to the next section. Hopefully, the short glossary at the back of the book will be of some assistance. For those who find the following too simple, my apologies and admiration.

NOTES:

1. *Hansard,* March 13, 2002. The same question was asked again a month later by another Member of Parliament and received a similar answer from the Prime Minister.

2. *Daily Telegraph,* March 20, 2002.

3. *Daily Telegraph,* March 16, 2002.

4. Previous books: *What is Love?* (Fount/Collins, 1977), *Secret Warriors* (Paternoster, 1984), *To God be the Glory* (Paternoster, 1986), *Paganism and the Occult* (Kingsway, 1988), *Close Encounters with the New Age* (Kingsway, 1991), *Satanism and the Occult* (Kingsway, 1994), *Joshua—Power to Win* (Kingsway, 1998), *Survival of the Fittest* (HarperCollins, 1999).

Chapter 2

Conflict Goes Worldwide

There is creation science and then there is real science. Such is the impatient majority view of Britain's white coats, following a decade of losses on the battlefield of public opinion. When "real scientists" are not being impatient, they try to stop themselves from crying by laughing at the funny side of what they see as "bad science." Creation science, they crack, is evolving, "mutating and spreading" like unwanted bacteria.[1]

The creationists are also smiling. Post-Darwinian society may have stripped them of their white coats and assigned them to the anorak brigade, but they are now fighting back. They claim to be the bearers of truth, unaffected by what David C. C. Watson called "The Great Brain Robbery" of evolution in his 1975 book.[2]

GLOBAL

"Forty-seven percent of Americans—and a quarter of college graduates—believe humans did not evolve, but were created by God a few thousand years ago," writes Debora Mackenzie in an edition of the *New Scientist.* She adds, "Nearly a third believe creationism should be taught in science lessons," as attempted by the education boards in the states of Kansas and Mississippi in modern times.

Proof enough of the rise of creationism is an edition of the leading science magazine almost completely devoted to explaining the phenomenon. "About time, too!" exclaimed one of the countless e-mails in the magazine's ensuing Web site debate. "The saddest edition ever," mourned another.[3]

> "Forty-seven percent of Americans—and a quarter of college graduates—believe humans did not evolve, but were created by God a few thousand years ago."

Nor is America isolated in its anti-evolutionary beliefs. It and Gateshead are in fact symbols of what is fast becoming a worldwide creationist revival. Australian students in Queensland are taught creation science. In Canada, there are more creationists per capita than anywhere else in the Western world, and creationism can be taught in every province. Incredibly, even Moscow has a thriving Creation Science Fellowship, and what they believe is taught in many state universities in Russia, probably in reaction to a fallen atheism whose intellectual foundation was, in part, evolution.

"In New Zealand," writes Debora Mackenzie, "creationists have gone from zero to a twentieth of the population in the past twenty-seven years." There is less startling, though still significant, growth in many parts of Africa, South America, the Indian sub-continent, and in Europe. Amazingly, evolution continued to be dismissed as "only a theory" in the Netherlands and did not make it into the graduation test papers in state schools until the turn of this millennium.

IN BRITAIN

Growth in Britain can be seen in the increase of societies and scientists supporting various forms of creation science.[4] However, it is hardly reflected in media or professional opinion—hence the outrage over Gateshead. Even leading religions have relegated evolution to the lower divisions of concern. The Church of England rarely mentions it, and the Pope has made public his acceptance of it.

A BBC Radio 4 millennium survey of Britain's leaders showed that 100 Church of England and Roman Catholic bishops did not accept the Genesis six-day creation. All but one scientist rejected it. Of the nearly 500 politicians, head teachers, scientists, and religious leaders who replied, only forty-six accepted Genesis in a literal way.

In surveys carried out for this book, 80 percent of Bible-believing evangelical Anglicans (at their annual conference) wanted to explain the Garden of Eden in terms other than literal. Hardly any evangelicals would have wished to do this a generation ago. Interestingly, the evangelical conference beliefs were almost the exact opposite to those of a large black Pentecostal church holding its away-weekend at the same venue and time.

A British survey in a typical northern evangelical parish showed a fifty-fifty split. In an average northern pub on quiz night, 85 percent checked options such as "the world wasn't made" and "life is an accident that came out of a Big Bang and a chance dance of chemicals." For the record, the survey was taken midevening before the full intake of alcohol.

However, even in Britain, there are signs that creation science is perhaps beginning to have influence. The *Church Times* 2002 survey recorded "a surprising level of doubt about evolution." Only 71 percent accepted it, with the remainder either against or uncertain.[5] Only 64 percent definitely believed it took God longer than six days for creation.

BATTLE LINES

Not surprisingly, this ideological and scientific war has many battle zones. We have so far identified the "for" and "against," but this is much too simplistic. In our pick-and-mix postmodern age, there are almost as many shades and sides as people. Most, however, would fit into four categories.

1. RECENT CREATION

God used a literal Genesis week to set up the universe between six and ten thousand years ago. Those who accept this in the

West are almost entirely Protestant evangelicals who believe that the Bible gives them no alternative. Those with scientific and philosophical training support their understanding of Scripture with what they see as strong extra-biblical evidence for a young earth (which we will investigate later). We include in this section an unknown number of Muslims, such as those in Turkey. They have, with permission, translated U.S. creationist books, replacing the biblical material with anti-Western slogans.[6]

In England, Muslim attitudes to a literal creation are optional among the large majority. The Qur'an has various levels of authority. The primary parts must be accepted by all. The secondary level—and this includes a literal view of creation—are left up to personal interpretation. However, those who run Muslim schools are of a more fundamentalist persuasion and may prefer to adopt the Gateshead line. Australian creationist John Mackay said on a U.K. tour, "This is not a phenomenon confined to Christianity. Islamic schools are equally if not more likely than Christian-faith schools to want to teach creation science."[7]

2. REMOTE CREATION

God took His time. Lots of it. The "days" of Genesis are seen as "epochs," modern science having provided the evidence for a new understanding of Scripture. The vast majority of Christians transferred into this area during the last two generations, assuring themselves of the old Galileo adage, that the Bible was written "not to show how the heavens go, but to show us how to go to heaven." They also took comfort from Francis Bacon's seventeenth-century idea of God's two books of truth—nature and Scripture—and the need to glean God's truth from both. Views in this section are many and varied, depending on how much God is thought to be involved in His evolving creation. Some are virtually deists, allowing God merely to set it all off before retiring for an early Sabbath rest. A second group wants God to be involved at the difficult stages, such as the transitions from nonlife to life, and from sea to land, and from land to air. They (people like Michael Behe) see God's necessary intervention in the unexplained complex areas as evidence for intelligent design. A final group (with writers like John Polkinghorne and Sam Berry) dislikes shoving a deity into the gaps of human knowledge and sees God as continually involved as a ground or foundation of evolving beings. They like to talk about the fine-tuning of the universe as indicating a divine presence.

This group feels angry towards the recent creationists, claiming that they stop people from taking the Bible seriously. The Bishop of Oxford, the Right Reverend Richard Harries, said, "If scientific truth suggests a particular hypothesis is the most likely one, I think it's quite wrong to reject this on dogmatic grounds. People need to look at the evidence."[8]

3. REVERENT AGNOSTICISM

The vast majority of our population appears to fall into this category. It is considered that the range of knowledge needed to reach an educated decision is so vast that most honest humans simply give up. Leading skeptic, as I write, is Steve Jones, Professor of Genetics at University College, London. In *Almost Like a Whale,* his much-acclaimed and highly readable rewrite of Darwin's *Origins,* Professor Jones often acknowledges the weaknesses in the argument for evolution, just as Darwin did. He is nevertheless an evolutionist while leaving himself open to persuasion of all arguments—except, of course, those of creation science.

In general, reverent agnostics know only one thing for certain: nothing can be known for certain. Consequently, they deem it right to follow whichever scientific "guru" explains it best. Hence, the Free Thinker's favorite entertainment is dabbling in bright ideas bubbling from *Star Trek* to science magazines to the latest documentary on the television. As I write, multiple universes are in vogue, and the already mentioned pub-quiz survey was strongly in favor. This states that we've hit the jackpot of eternity as the products of the one universe in a billion that just happened to produce and evolve life. Alternatively, we just happen to live in the one universe, parallel to at least ten others, that can support life as we know it. (Ten? Don't ask. That's another book, at least.) *Star Trek*, especially in *The Next Generation*, took most of its ideas from the various vogues and fashions of science.

Reverent agnostics are ultimately the products of the modern information revolution. They are faced with a worldwide Internet of knowledge. It can and does lead searchers to information, and therefore help with decisions. But for many, it is too much. The glut overwhelms them, and they lose their ability—and therefore shrug off the responsibility—to know anything for certain.

4. RELIGIOUS ATHEISM

This is the firm belief that we are products of a simple, uncreated, and accidental recipe—an algorithm. This is the proposal in Daniel Dennett's book *Darwin's Dangerous Idea.*[9] This mechanical formula for life had to occur sooner or later. There was no escaping it. Richard Dawkins would want to add that these "neutral and mindless" foolproof recipes of Dennett's produce selfish genes, existing only to reproduce. Professor Dawkins relishes dismantling creation science and debunks its favorite design argument in *The Blind Watchmaker.* Christian thinker William Paley had maintained that just as a watch must have had a designer, so we can deduce that the much more complex world also has a supreme designer. Not so, insists Professor Dawkins. It is all the product of a blind recipe. Religious atheists are, of course, similar to the group at the other end of our spectrum, each being fundamentalist and wanting to evangelize. The fundamental with recent creationists is their belief that Genesis must be interpreted literally. The fundamental with religious atheists is, of course, their belief that there is no God.

This last group breaks down into two rival camps. Those like Dawkins and Dennett (and many others) insist that they already have the full explanation of how everything evolved. Natural selection or survival of the fittest sums it up neatly. The opposing camp (populated by people like Michael Denton, the late Stephen Gould, Niles Eldredge, plus many others) believes that natural selection is not so amazing. It only partly explains evolution. Some other cause, either not known or one of their own pet theories, is what is missing.

These, then, are the four armies in our war, though we are still being too simplistic. Battle lines are often blurred, and there is no well-defined "no-man's land" between each force, except between creation science and the rest. Also, there is often much joining of forces, especially when groups want to reinforce each other against creation science.

Understanding this warfare is only possible by taking a brief trip through time. It is a fascinating and revealing journey and is not always what popular opinion expects. Surprising twists and turns are revealed as we examine two of the major battle lines drawn up between the Old Earthers and the Young Earthers.

NOTES:

1. *New Scientist,* April 22, 2000.

2. David C. C. Watson, *The Great Brain Robbery* (Walter, 1975).

3. *New Scientist,* April 22, 2000.

4. Among the leading groups against evolution are: Creation Science Movement, P.O. Box 888, Portsmouth, PO6 2YD, U.K.; Answers in Genesis (U.K.), P.O. Box 5262, Leicester LE2 3XU, U.K.; Biblical Creation Society, P.O. Box 22, Rugby CV22 7SY, U.K.; and Creation Resources Trust, Mead Farm, Downhead, West Camel, Yeovil BA22 7RQ, U.K. There is a host of Web sites available through entering "creation" and "evolution" in your search engines.

5. *Church Times,* January 25, 2002.

6. *New Scientist,* April 22, 2000.

7. *Church Times,* "Bishops Speak Up for Evolution," March 21, 2002.

8. Ibid.

9. Daniel C. Dennett, *Darwin's Dangerous Idea* (Penguin Press, 1995), 48–50.

❖ EVOLUTION OF THE EARTH

Chapter 3

Old Earthers

Just how old is Father Time on earth? Know this and agree on it, and a cease-fire could be declared overnight. All sides could shake hands and get a life. All we need to do is reconcile a Father Time in diapers with the stooped geriatric who brandishes an hourglass and scythe. Is he a few billion years old? If so, there's plenty of time for evolution. Is he merely a few thousand years old? In that case, only a special creation, or something like it, will do.

There now follows two brief histories of time—Old Earthers and Young Earthers—in the next two chapters. Again, we'll try to avoid the vitriol of the sort that tends to have each accusing the other of thinking like Flat Earthers.

OLD EARTH

A few ancient Greeks and the occasional genius like Leonardo da Vinci had glimmers while messing around with minerals and fossils, but nothing caught the imagination timewise. The first to hang a date on beginnings was Archbishop James Ussher of Armagh. In the 1650s, this renowned biblical scholar published his Old Testament chronology, setting October 4004 B.C. as the month of creation. His offering might have sunk without notice except it was anointed with a biblical sanctity. Editions of the King James Version of the Bible began to include it in the margins.

> It must therefore have taken millions of years to produce the landscape he now worked and walked on.

It was to be another century before Scottish farmer James Hutton began to take note of land formations and nature's wear-and-tear processes. He observed sediments, produced by weathering, being taken down and deposited in the sea. His genius was to jump from such slim evidence to mind-boggling geological epochs. He reasoned that the same processes he saw working in his day must be uniformly the same as in the past. It must therefore have taken millions of years to produce the landscape he now worked and walked on. Mr. Hutton's central idea came to be known as "uniformitarianism," though he probably never used the term himself. Simply put, the key to understanding the past was in the processes of the present.

"Heresy!" cried his critics, brought up on Ussher and the Genesis Flood, which was unlike anything happening in their present. "Ridiculous!" dismissed followers of French naturalist Georges Cuvier. He claimed there was nothing uniform about the catastrophes of a planet ravaged by earthquakes and floods. His followers were called the "catastrophists."

The battle raged on, not helped by Hutton's poor writing. He could read the planet but couldn't easily plant ideas in his readers. Few understood until, in the 1830s, Charles Lyell's persuasive *Principles of Geology* hit the bookstands, and this, an extensive and readable development of Hutton's thinking, quickly weaned the main thinkers away from catastrophes. Uniformitarianism won the age.

William Smith also helped. In 1815, he produced an underground snapshot of England and Wales, having peeked below the surface during the mad rush to network the nation with canals. He trekked the freshly excavated trenches, noting that fossils of different types were in different layers. Always, the same specific fossil could be found in the same specific rock, whether the outcrops of rock were yards apart or miles apart. He concluded that they must have been the same rock, laid down at the same time and in the same conditions. Each different point was carefully noted; then he simply joined up the dots to produce his map.

Hutton may have fathered modern geology, but it came of age with Smith. The map of underground strata met the acid test of science. It was testable. He often amazed his friends with his geological guessing games. While out walking, he'd spy outcrops in the distance and be able to predict exactly what they would find on arrival. Geology became so predictable that coal, oil, and gold could be found with accuracy.

And all this spoke of great geological ages. This was confirmed later by the dating game and ...

RADIOMETRIC TECHNIQUES

In the early twentieth century, Ernest Rutherford first suggested that newly discovered radioactivity could be used to date rocks. However, it was Arthur Holmes, who was in the right place at Imperial College at the right time (around 1906, a decade after the discovery of radioactivity), and who developed the earth's built-in clocks.

All radioactive elements, like thorium, uranium, or carbon-14, decay at set rates into different forms. They lose (emit) particles (alpha or beta) or rays (gamma) from the nucleus. Each element has a half-life—the period in which it loses half its activity by decay. Carbon-14 has a half-life of 5,730 years, while uranium-238's half-life is four-and-a-half billion years.

Therefore, establishing the decay stage of elements in the rocks provided an approximate date when the rocks were formed. The oldest rock Arthur Holmes dated, using the uranium-lead technique, was 1.6 billion years. This staggered the scientific community, then firmly settled on an earth age of 100 million years. Radiometric dating now includes carbon-14, potassium-argon, rubidium-strontium, plus methods involving thorium-230 and lead, and the list goes on.

We now move to areas that might not be "clocks," but indicate huge geological eras.

PLATE TECTONICS

Jigsaw enthusiasts spotted it immediately. The only thing that stopped South America fitting snugly into the coastlines of Africa was the Atlantic. Could it be that once they were one?

German geophysicist Alfred Wegener and others thought so, and, supported by more circumstantial evidence, he presented his theory in 1912. He couldn't provide a mechanism for his cruising continents, just the take-it-or-leave-it courage of his own observations.

Science had to wait for plate tectonics and deep-seafloor exploration in the 1960s to provide the theoretical means of propulsion. According to this hypothesis, we live on half a dozen continental-sized "floating" platforms, or plates, that extend down eighteen to ninety miles. This was worked out from "sonic body scans" of the earth, taken as the belt of monitoring stations measured the great seismic energy of earthquakes.

The scans revealed a central core the size of Mars, made up of iron and nickel. There was an outer core, surrounded by a mantle. Floating on top was the scum, or crust. At one level, there was "a weak layer" that could become "fluid," rather like present-day glass. Our "windows" are in flux, moving tiny fractions over hundreds of years. This thixotropic speed, making a snail look like a derby winner, allows the top part of the mantle and the crust to break off from the lower part of the mantle, and thus move about.

This was intricately linked with seafloor spreading from midocean ridges, a phenomenon only observed in detail after U.S. Defense submariners got tired of bumping into things and so decided to map the ocean floors with echo-measuring sonar. This, together with shipborne magnetometric sweeps across midocean ridges, showed that the seabeds on either side of the ridges were mirror images of each other. They showed similar magnetic patterns. The nearer the rocks were to the ridge, the younger they were. They measured seabed sediment. It was absent at the newly created sides of the ridge but then went deeper the farther away the seabed was. This indicated a gradual spreading over vast ages.

The hypothesis of Pangaea is closely associated with continental drift. Pangaea was a superland thought to cover a third of the planet before breaking up 200 million years ago to drift into the present-day continental alignments.

FLIPPING POLES

From time to time, the earth's magnetic poles flip. The north becomes the south, and vice versa. This shows up in strata and beds with contradictory polarizations. We already hinted at this earlier, when discussing magnetic patterns, but it is worth highlighting separately.

Underwater pole anomalies were first detected by submarine sonar in the Second World War. They weren't understood until the discovery of pole flipping in 1960. As the sea floor spread from midocean ridges, the rocks solidified and were imprinted with the then magnetic pole. What submarines picked up were the bands with varying magnetic pole prints, showing that they had been laid down and "conveyored" into position over huge geological ages.

All this thinking caused a mid-twentieth-century revolution in geological thinking, confirming beyond doubt, for the vast majority, that Father Time on earth was indeed old—4.6 billion years old, to be (fairly) precise.

WHAT ABOUT 4004 B.C.?

Archbishop Ussher and his Young Earth date had met their match long before this. The archbishop's ideas were quietly set aside, especially by the church. Even the great Bible commentators were won over to believe that God's initial act of creation had been at least several hundred thousand years before their nineteenth century, and this without the extra evidence of plate tectonics and seafloor spreading.

This didn't stop them from taking Genesis literally. They did this with the help of a divine period at the end of the first verse. The Gap Theory, they called it. "In the beginning God created the heavens and the earth." This was followed by a huge gap to accommodate all the geological ages then being discovered. "Now the earth was formless and empty, darkness was over the surface of the deep, and the Spirit of God was hovering over the waters."

More of this theory in chapter 16. Here, we note that it did help Bible commentators to persuade many in pulpits and pews that Archbishop Ussher had erred. This was especially true when one of his successors at Canterbury, John

Bird Sumner, described in print how geology and Genesis could be harmonized.

GEOLOGICAL AGES

We cannot leave the Old Earth cause without a brief trip down those famous geological ages. A reminder of them will also help us to understand the case of the Young Earthers.

Radioactivity, it is claimed, has helped to establish "absolute ages," in millions of years, for the various geological epochs. The divisions largely relate to the fossilized remains of living things found in them, and because life only exploded on earth in the last tenth of the earth's history, the two great geological divisions reflect this. First, the Precambrian or the Cryptozoic (hidden life). Elementary life was present towards the end of this age but left little fossil evidence. Second, the Cambrian or the Phanerozoic (obvious life). This is further divided into the classical periods below.

Note: Three massive geological changes are said to have happened as we unfold the geological ages.

1. The super continent of Rodinia (centered on the South Pole) breaks up.

2. Large chunks of Rodinia (Gondwanaland and Laurasia) merge into the huge pole-to-pole continent of Pangaea.

3. Pangaea disintegrates into the present-day continents.

GEOLOGIC COLUMN

❖ Cambrian (570–500 million years ago). Invertebrate life explodes in the sea. Lots of trilobites. No land life.

❖ Ordovician (500–430). Trilobites still number one with corals catching up, plus early vertebrates, and primitive jawless fish with armor.

❖ Silurian (430–395). Bad news: trilobites have had their heyday. Good news: some fish have now got jaws. Corals cover the globe. Life comes ashore— simple plants with their own built-in, do-it-yourself plumbing.

❖ Devonian (395–345). Devonian rocks abound with fresh water and sea-fish fossils, jawed and jawless. True jaws arrive with the first shark. Land boringly covered by giant ferns. Début for spiral-shelled ammonites. Trilobite decline continues.

❖ Carboniferous (345–280). Land life explodes into lush forests. Major coal beds are laid. Amphibians give rise to reptiles and the prototype dragonfly takes off in formation with other fledgling insects.

❖ Permian (280–225). First real conifers take root. The great Pangaea now forming. Land upheaval causes mass extinction. Farewell swim for the trilobites. Ammonites also look doomed.

❖ Triassic (225–195). The Paleozoic (ancient life) comes to an end. Curtain rises on the Mesozoic (middle life)— primarily the age of the reptile. The first dinosaurs and turtles appear, plus mammals. Ammonites stage recovery before another slump.

❖ Jurassic (195–136). T-Rex rules and giant dinosaurs roam. First primitive birds reach for the sky (or jump up and down a lot from trees). Crabs and lobsters appear.

❖ Cretaceous (136 to 65 million years ago). Dinosaurs killed off. Prime suspect is a large meteorite causing global catastrophe and climate change. Earth finally gets the hang of flower arranging and puts on magnificent show. Ammonites lose the will to live.

❖ Tertiary (65 to 2.5 million years ago). Cenozoic (recent life) period begins. Life forms become more like those of today. Golden age for mammals. The Eocene epoch sees new mammal groups from mini-horses to whales. The Oligocene epoch produces dogs and cats. The Miocene brings marsupials and humanlike apes. Placental mammals make it big in Pliocene.

❖ Quaternary (2.5 million to present day). Many continental ice sheets. Prehumans somewhere in south-central Africa, China, and Java (Lower and Mid-Pleistocene). Homo sapiens arrive in later Pleistocene. Ice sheets retreat. Modern humanity thrives.

EMBROIDERY AGE

We need to take care. The above is, of course, not all absolute fact. It is the product of the dating game, fossil hunts, leapfrogging from one logic to another, educated inspiration, genius, and guesses.

Nor should we forget our tendency to embroider. The British have a breakfast cereal television commercial that has homo-something-or-other, increasingly unbending in his posture, until he becomes bright and upright enough to reach for his cereal. Such a sequence is fun to show B.C. man—Before Cornflakes—but, of course, it is a picture that exists nowhere outside the minds of marketing gurus and fantasy scientists.

And remember what we can do with a jawbone and a few other bits and pieces. The bone ends up on the television with legs and long, hairy arms, and with its own family and community in its own hour-long prehistoric soap. All this from a few shards of bone and flint tools.

And then there's the digitally enhanced T-Rex behaving like a forty-five-mile-per-hour Jurassic Park Roadrunner. The poor fellow's weight-to-muscle-to-oxygen ratio would have put his top sprint at a lumbering asthmatic stroll. So too would his short arms. A mad dash through the jungle, an accidental trip, and poor T-Rex would have crushed himself to death without arms to cushion his fall.

All of which prepares us for the other side of the argument—the Young Earthers. Surely they cannot mount any credible case after our tour de force on the age of the earth. Can they really expect the whole of modern science to rewrite itself to suit a literal reading of some ancient text? "The Christian who believes that the idea of an ancient earth is unbiblical," writes Davis A. Young, "would do better to deny the validity of any kind of historical geology and insist that the rocks must be the product of pure miracle rather than to explain them in terms of

the flood. An examination of the earth apart from ideological pre-
suppositions is bound to lead to the conclusion that it is ancient."[1]
    Well, let's see.

NOTE:

1. Davis A. Young, *Portraits of Creation* (Eerdmans, 1990).

Chapter 4

Young Earthers

The case for the Old Earthers rests. Like many juries at this stage, you wonder why on earth you were ever called to adjudicate. Isn't it an open-and-shut case? What could the defense possibly say against such overwhelming evidence? "Plenty!" the Young Earthers might exclaim.

However, the creationists don't make it easy. It's no wonder few take notice of them. They have so many geological models, and some even contradict each other. Against this disunited front, it is no wonder that mainstream geology is winning by a landslide. Creationist writer Malcolm Bowden explained to me about geology in general and then creationists in particular:

> The problem is that each geologist will inter-
> pret strata in his own way, according to the

model he holds to … creationists also differ strongly amongst themselves. So you will have to come to your own conclusions, as there is no generally accepted model for geology among creationists. It is the most difficult subject to interpret in accordance with the biblical account.

The following, then, is a digest from several sources of the young earth argument.

Of course, it rests squarely on a Genesis worldwide deluge causing much of what we now observe on our planet. Slow formation of some strata plus the effects of erosion are accepted, but only since the Genesis flood. Young Earthers insist that present-day evidence shows that strata and today's geological phenomena do not need huge geological ages in which to form. Often these can appear rapidly in hours or days or years. The Young Earthers use many case studies to prove their point. We will limit ourselves here to two favorites—the Grand Canyon and the Mount St. Helens' eruption.

> Young Earthers insist that present-day evidence shows that strata and today's geological phenomena do not need huge geological ages in which to form.

THE GRAND CANYON

It's up to a mile deep. Its incredible buttes, spires, and cliffs are a picture postcard of our past, and any sightseer can admire the different layers, beds, and strata. The big question is, of course, how were the beds made?

Scientific orthodoxy states that the Colorado River took between seven and thirty-six million years to carve out this natural museum of fairly recent geology.

Young Earthers, such as those from the Institute for Creation Research, beg to disagree at their permanent Grand Canyon research center near Flagstaff, Arizona. They, and hundreds of others on field trips, maintain that all the layers can be accounted for by one or more of three explanations of a worldwide Genesis-type flood. These indicate how bedrock was tilted between Creation and Flood, and how the dozen or so other sedimentary rock layers were laid horizontally on top of each other, first as the waters rose, then as they receded, and afterwards.[1]

They would further point out:

1. Strata include the fossils of animals according to their habitat and mobility. In other words, the simpler life forms in the lower strata are there because they were not able to climb out of danger as did higher life forms. It has nothing to do with the Old Earther claims that only simpler life forms were alive when the strata were laid.

2. The canyon may have appeared as quickly as one century after the flood laid down the many strata. When the initial crack appeared, the various sedimentary layers would have solidified.

An earthquake or some other catastrophe could have opened it up initially, while erosion and the Colorado River added the finishing touches.

3. There are forests of conifers in many strata, yet according to uniformitarian orthodoxy, conifers did not evolve until after the top layer was in place.

4. There are the missing strata. If each was laid one on top of the other, why are half the strata in the Grand Canyon (as in other places) missing? More than a billion years is missing. Erosion is to blame, the geologists say. But can a thousand million years of the earth's history be washed away, and written off so easily?

MOUNT ST. HELENS

It blew its top and one side on May 18, 1980, with the force of 20,000 Hiroshima-sized atom bombs. The Institute of Creation Research scientists spent three summers investigating the geological changes, writes Dr. Steve Austin, and they found that four geological phenomena, usually associated with uniformitarianism, were caused by this sudden catastrophe.[2]

1. Rapidly formed stratification. Strata nearly 400 feet high have formed during the volcano's activity. "A deposit accumulated in less than one day, on June 12, 1980, is 25 feet thick and contains many thin laminae and beds," writes Dr. Austin. "Conventionally, sedimentary laminae and beds are assumed to represent longer seasonal variations, or annual changes, as the

layers accumulated very slowly. Mount St. Helens teaches us that the stratified layers commonly characterizing geological formations can form rapidly by flow processes."

2. Rapid erosion. This lends support to their Grand Canyon theory. Among the many geological changes caused by air blast, landslide, and pyroclastic flows, one mudflow eroded a nearby canyon system up to 140 feet deep in the headwaters of the North Fork of the Toutle River Valley in one day—March 19, 1982. The little "Grand Canyon" is a one-fortieth scale model of the real Grand Canyon. "The small creeks ... of the Toutle River today," writes Dr. Austin, "might seem, by appearances, to have carved these canyons very slowly over a long period." Mount St. Helens has shown them the catastrophic alternative.

3. Upright deposited logs. In Yellowstone National Park and elsewhere, upright trees have been petrified at various levels. Normal uniformitarian geology interprets these as multiple forests that grew on different levels over thousands of years. However, 19,000 upright tree stumps existed on the floor of Spirit Lake after being blown there in the Mount St. Helens' blast (upright because waterlogged trees eventually sink "root ball" first). Five years after the blast, scuba divers noted that as the stumps reached the lakeshore, they were trapped by sediment forming around their roots. Others were still floating free at different levels. This process had occurred over two decades rather than thousands of years.

4. Peat layer in Spirit Lake. Coal, according to uniformitarians, takes thousands of years to form. "The Spirit Lake

peat … is texturally very similar to coal," writes Dr. Austin. "All that is needed is burial and slight heating to transform the Spirit Lake peat into coal." And this would only take a matter of years.

Young Earthers see Mount St. Helens as a "miniature laboratory" for catastrophism. In some respects, "Mount St. Helens helps us to imagine what the biblical flood of Noah's day may have been like," concludes Dr. Austin.

UNIFORMITARIANS VS. CATASTROPHISTS

Young Earthers refer often to uniformitarianism. They are determined to win victory and prove once and for all that the earth could not have slowly evolved.

We need to pause for a moment in the name of fairness. You will have noticed that Young Earthers refer often to uniformitarianism. They are determined to win victory and prove once and for all that the earth could not have slowly evolved. Meanwhile, the Old Earthers wonder what all the fuss is about.

It is time we set this battle in its true context.

Young Earthers often see mainstream geology following in the uniformitarian footsteps of Lyell and disciples, and attack them for doing so. Modern secular geologists are mystified, even angry, at this. They insist that all geologists trained in the last generation have accepted a mixture of catastrophism and uniformitarianism. They have been doing this ever since Luis Alvarez in 1980 posed the mass extinction of dinosaurs by a large asteroid.

In fact, even before this, as far back as 1924, catastrophism began to reemerge after the initial reaction against it by Lyell and his followers. The 1924 Grand Banks earthquake off Canada proved a revelation. Incredibly, vast deposits of mud were laid down in a matter of hours. A massive wedge of mud was sent slithering and crashing off the continental shelf and down into the deep basin of the North Atlantic at fifty miles per hour. The speed was calculated from the successive snapping of thirteen transatlantic cables. The mud spread over a hundred thousand square miles to a depth of two to three feet. It did it all in thirteen hours.

THIRTEEN HOURS

This began a quiet revolution among some geologists that culminated in modern geology happily embracing catastrophe in the 1980s. Many now believe that Hutton and Lyell's uniformitarianism properly understood the relevence of volcanoes and other catastrophes. When Hutton said that the key to understanding the past was in the present, he was taking the eruptions and catastrophes of his day into account.

This is highly debatable, and it takes a very kind view of their motives and thinking. However, what is true today is that mainstream geology changed its ways certainly a generation ago and took catastrophism firmly on board.

As a result, modern geology looks at the Mount St. Helens' explosion and sees no problem whatsoever in strata forming suddenly. It can even accept the odd minor catastrophe happening in the formation of the Grand Canyon (depending on which geologist you talk to). Twenty-first-century geology has recovered from its historic hangovers and is happy to take on board what is to be learned from catastrophe.

That said, it does not mean that the Young Earthers have no case. It just makes their argument less clear-cut. Every time they argue for sudden strata, for instance, modern geology agrees. Young Earthers, however, believe they are on safer ground with some of the following.

SALTY SEAS

"Why is the sea salty?" asked S. Ord of Durham, a reader of *The Sunday Telegraph's* question and answer science column.[3] Science Editor Robert Matthews gave the standard reply: "The mystery is not so much why is the sea salty, but more why isn't it packed with the stuff?"

Erosion has dumped the raw ingredients for common salt—chlorine and sodium ions—into the oceans at the ratio of four teaspoons to each pint of sea water. Matthews said that this concentration, "if it were extracted … would cover our planet with a layer of salt 150 ft. thick." At this rate, every ocean in the world should be as saturated with salt as the Dead Sea. Obviously they are not. Why not?

Creationists insist that the low concentrations of salt, not to mention the lower-than-expected levels of all other ocean chemicals, give a much younger age for the earth.

COMET LIFESPANS

Comets like Hale-Bopp and Halley will not return one day. Their comet tails tell of their steady disintegration every time they orbit near the sun. One day, they will be no more—melted snowballs. Comets have a typical life span of around 10,000 years.[4]

Old Earthers have proposed a sort of "comet factory" called the Oort Cloud, somewhere far beyond Pluto's orbit. It can't be observed, nor indeed can the complicated collision process of passing stars that is supposed to dislodge the comets. Other Old Earthers rely on the Kuiper Belt, thought to be much nearer Pluto. Again, this has not been observed. It also needs the Oort Cloud to feed it. Creationists say that "comet factories" are inventions by desperate evolutionists.[5]

POPULATION POSER

In chapter 11, we will examine the claim that Homo sapiens have been around for 150,000 years. Young Earthers suggest this is impossible: if that were the case, the human race would by now not have enough room on the planet.

Old Earthers say this is nonsense: countless factors and laws guiding population statistics, involving plague, disease, pestilence, war and natural catastrophe, food shortages and man-made disasters have all kept the numbers in check. As I write, Marc Reichow of the University of Leicester and his colleagues report that a vast flood of magma gushing from Russia's Siberian platform killed off "90 percent of species in the oceans and 70 percent on the land."[6] Admittedly, this was 200 million years before humans, and precise percentages need to be taken with a large pinch of salt at this time scale, but it nevertheless points to large-scale extinction. Old Earthers also insist that there must have been times when the human race failed to grow. Again as I write, British families are now producing fewer children than any time since records began.[7]

However, Young Earthers say that their statistics take normal population fluctuations into account. They cite the figures for two nations:

1. Britain. Statistician Paul Nicholls for the Creation Science Movement shows that the lowest rate of growth in Great Britain since 1801 was just under half a percent a year.[8] This growth rate occurred despite losing millions in world wars, famine, genocide, and plague. Overall, the growth rate from 1801 to the 1991 census was 0.87 percent a year.

Nicholls asks his readers to consider eight survivors stepping ashore after the Genesis flood about, say, 4,400 years ago. How long would it have taken them to expand into the world's 1991 population?

At the lowest growth rate (just under half a percent a year), it would have taken 4,738 years. At the average growth rate (0.87 percent a year) it would have taken 2,347 years.

What, then, would be the population after 150,000 years?

2. The Jews. A 3,860-year slice from the history of the world's most persecuted and punished race is offered for analysis by Young Earthers Professor H. Enoch and E. R. Thiele.[9] They use the known generations and numbers between the father of Israel, Jacob (in 1930 B.C.), to A.D. 1930 when the population of world Jewry was 16 million. This showed that the Jewish population had doubled twenty-four times, which worked out at once every 161 years. They also worked out the doubling rate of the whole human race (from the time of a Genesis-type flood) and this came to a remarkably similar 160 years.

Professor Enoch then invited his readers to examine the evolutionary hypothesis using a notional Genesis flood date of 2519 B.C.:

> If we push back the date of our ancestors by as little as 1,600 years (and deny the fact of the Flood, as evolutionists do), we must multiply the present world population by $2^{10} = 1,024$—more than a thousandfold!
>
> If we double that time (3,200) and add it to the Flood date 2519 B.C. (thus postulating 5719 B.C. as the birthday of Homo sapiens), then the present population would be one million times as great as it is today.

This compares favorably with the trend of figures used earlier by Paul Nicholls. There would have been enough human beings today to fill not only this planet, but countless others besides.

Is all this completely rubbish, as Old Earthers maintain? Do we dismiss it as useless in the light of the laws of population, or is there something in it?

The Young Earthers think the next point underlines their insistence that it should be considered.

WHERE HAVE ALL THE SKELETONS GONE?

Anthropologists say that the population of Neanderthal and Cro-Magnon man was between one and ten million for up to 100,000 years. All this time they were burying bodies plus artifacts—that's at least four billion bodies, each with artifacts. Even if the bones didn't last, the artifacts would have—four billion sets of artifacts!

> The trouble we have at this stage, despite all the scientific data, is one of beliefs and worldviews. Both views contain an element of faith.

What has been found so far suggests a history for Neanderthal and Cro-Magnon men of a few hundred years rather than 100,000 years.[10]

THE CAVEMAN PAINTINGS

We're told, say Young Earthers, that Stone Age man made beautiful cave paintings. They kept records of the moon's phases.

They built great monuments, like Stonehenge. Why then wait a hundred thousand years before using the same skills to start writing their own history and developing modern civilization?[11]

The same argument can be made for agriculture. Why did such clever men and women wait 100,000 years before getting down to farming?

AND THE REST

This Young Earthers list goes on and on. There should be much more helium in places. Many strata are too tightly bent. Injected sandstone shortens geological ages. Fossil radioactivity shortens geological ages to a few years. Earth's magnetic field is decaying too fast. It could never have lasted millions of years.

All this, say Young Earthers, points to a young earth.

But what about the dates? What about the millions, even billions, of years we keep hearing about?

Consequently, the trouble we have at this stage, despite all the scientific data, is one of beliefs and worldviews. Both views contain an element of faith. This, of course, is furiously denied by atheistic Old Earthers. But the truth does seem to be inescapable. How you interpret some of this data will depend on your belief system.

These faith positions are even more evident in the dating game, which we will look at next.

NOTES:

1. Assessments of a young earth Grand Canyon can be obtained from any creation society Web site (simply enter "creationists" in your search engine). Old-earth views are well laid out by Howard J. Van Till (and others) in *Portraits of Creation* (Eerdmans, 1990), and *Science Held Hostage* (InterVarsity Press, 1988).

2. Steven A. Austin, *Mount St. Helens and Catastrophism* (Creation Science Movement, 1990).

3. *The Sunday Telegraph,* May 26, 2002.

4. P. F. Steidl, *Planets, Comets, and Asteroids, Design and Origins,* ed. G. Mulfinger (Creation Research Society Books, 1983).

5. www.christiananswers.net. "Evidence for a young world."

6. *Science Journal,* June 5, 2002.

7. Government population figures, May 2002.

8. Paul Nicholls, *Population Growth*, Pamphlet 301 (Creation Science Movement, 1995).

9. Professor H. Enoch, *Evolution or Creation?* (Evangelical Press, 1976), 86–89. Also, E. R. Thiele, *The Mysterious Numbers of Hebrew Kings,* 1951.

10. As note 5, p. 3.

11. J. O. Dritt, "Exploring the Mind of Ice Age Man in the Evolutionary Timetable." Address to 1990 Creation Science Fellowship, pp. 73–78.

Chapter 5

The Dating Game

This is no game for the sensitive. Finding the age of rocks has put years on those who do it, splitting more colleagues, relationships, and creation societies than any other subject.

Dating is often viewed as the core of our controversy. One leading Young Earther, a dermatologist with the quixotic name of Molleurus Couperus, believed that evolution stood or fell on "the determination of the age of the various layers and the age of the contained fossils by their radioactivity and helium content."[1] The whole of geology and modern science would agree. They abide by the long-established rules of the dating game, and the media are also happy to report it, with headlines such as "300-million-year-old fossilized dragonfly found in a coal," or whatever.

Science is at home with dating because it is based, it insists, on solid data from the real world. It meets the tests of empiricism—the gaining of knowledge solely via observation and experiment. Geologists can show that elements and their atoms have measurable properties and behave in measurable ways. They size, weigh, describe, and, above all, predict the way in which they will behave by the way they have behaved in the past.

Young Earthers, like Couperus and the growing number of modern counterparts, would agree with all of the above except the last nine words.

"How can we possibly know how they have behaved in the past?" would be their collective challenge. Specifically on radiometric dating, how can science know for sure that its earth clocks have been "running at the same rate throughout past years?" queries professor D. B. Gower. "This is really the Theory of Uniformitarianism—that the rate at which things are happening has been constant from the beginning."[2]

The professor adds a second requirement for dating: "Some idea must be obtained as to how tightly the 'clock' was wound initially (e.g., when using the depth of cosmic dust, as in a geochronometer, it is important to know if a layer was present initially)." Old Earthers, on the other hand, are ready and willing to show just exactly how tightly wound the clocks are. They have their well-tried methods.

But, hold the controversy. We are too early into the fray. We need a quick neutral tour of our subject to make sure we grasp what each side is fighting for.

THE DATING METHOD

Rocks contain many chemical elements, most of which are stable. Iron will stay iron no matter how long the universe lasts. Some, however, change. Atoms of uranium, carbon, potassium, rubidium, and the like decay into other elements, and they do so at known rates. A rock's age can therefore be gauged by checking the radioactive decay.

But before that, a quick checkup on our basics. An atom of these elements is, to put it crudely, like a tiny solar system with planets (electrons) circling a sun (the nucleus). The nucleus itself is made up of smaller units or particles called neutrons and protons. If you could enlarge an atom to the size of Wimbledon's tennis stadium, the nucleus and its particles would be smaller than a pint-sized basket of strawberries.

That would be some enlargement! The largest atom weighs 0.000 000 000 000 000 000 004 grams. To save working in these mind-boggling micronumbers, the weight or mass of an atom is worked off of a standard atom of carbon, which is given as 12. This gives the lightest element, hydrogen, an atomic weight of 1. The heaviest is uranium at 238.

John Dalton, on discovering the atomic world, stated that "atoms of the same element are alike in every respect, and atoms of different elements differ in shape, size, weight (mass), and general behavior." What he didn't know and what we've since discovered is that the atoms can be changed into different atoms: parent elements can be changed into daughter elements at a predictable rate. Elements can decay through a steady stream of what are called alpha particles, beta particles, and gamma rays. These result from the activities of particles in the atom. This can cause neutrons to be added or sub-tracted, thereby creating an isotope (or variety/daughter) of an element.

Many isotopes decay into other elements as they radiate alpha or beta particles or gamma rays, and these can be measured. The decay curve of an isotope can be drawn to show its half-life—when 50 percent of the isotope has been lost. After a further equal time, half of the remainder will be lost, and so on.

Old Earthers swear by these clocks. Young Earthers give the impression that they want to swear at them, if they could allow themselves.

Here are the main points of disagreement between the two parties:

1. HALF-LIFE SUSPECT

The half-life of an isotope may not always have been what it is today. "There is much evidence," writes professor Gower, "to indicate that the 'half-lives' of isotopes are associated with cosmic ray bombardment (i.e. neutron bombardment) from outer space ... thus, although the 'half-life' may be constant in the laboratory, there is no guarantee that it will remain so in a rock that is open to the elements." In this case, stress Young Earthers, today's rock dates might be millions of years out.

Dr. Roger C. Wiens, of the Los Alamos National Laboratory, denies this. Writing a Christian perspective on radiometric dating, he says, "There are only three quite technical instances where a half-life changes, and these do not affect the dating techniques." Cosmic rays, he insists, are very high-energy atomic nuclei flying through space and can only affect half-life at slow speeds. Even then, they would only do it by a couple of percent. Instead of 100,000 years, it would be 102,000 years.[3]

2. A FALSE START

The original amount of the radioactive substance (the amount present immediately after crystallization of the mineral) cannot be known, say Young Earthers. The "clock" may have had a false time to start with. No scientists were around to measure it when crystallization occurred. "What if it were formed by some other (or additional) mechanism?" asks professor Gower. "What if the product itself were lost to a greater or lesser extent from the mineral, or, alternatively, the concentration of the initial isotope varied with weathering conditions?" Again, the accuracy of dating would be suspect.

But, again, Old Earthers retaliate. They stress that they do know the original makeup of rocks, plus the level of original radioactive material. They have their isochron diagram. The technically minded can visit the notes on this one. Here, in the main text, we keep it simple.[4] The isochron plots present levels of radioactive parent and daughter isotopes and compares them with the element's unchanging stable isotope. These points are plotted on a diagram and they point to the original makeup of the rock. At least, that was the case until recently. Creationist geologist Paul Garner says that isochrons have been shown to contradict each other:

> What does this tell us about isochron dating?
> Well, geologists are coming round to the idea
> that isochron dating is not all that it's cracked
> up to be. I have a paper, published in *Chemical*

Geology in 1989, and Dr. Zeng here says, "As
it is impossible to distinguish a valid isochron
from an apparent isochron … caution must be
taken … in explaining the … age of any geological system." So the isochron method is
falling into disrepute, certainly in some areas.[5]

The creationists' third charge is that the makeup of the
"clocks" themselves might be faulty.

3. POTASSIUM-ARGON LEAKAGE

The potassium-argon dating method is questionable.
Potassium-40 in rocks changes into argon-40 (11 percent) and
calcium-40 (89 percent). The calcium is useless for measure-
ment because there is already too much calcium in rock. But
argon-40 is also not without its problems according to Professor
Gower and many others.

❖ Argon as a gas "can diffuse easily from rocks, depending on the porosity of the surface, and on prevailing
pressure. Thus rocks deeper in the earth crust, where
pressure is high, will lose argon to rocks nearer to the
surface."[6] Other similar problems will tend to show surface rock as being of a greater age than it actually is.

❖ Potassium is easily washed out of minerals due to the
high solubility of its salts. In that case, potassium will
have a reduced presence, indicating that it is older than
it actually is.

❖ Potassium in volcanic rock is particularly problematic.
This type of rock picks it up from the potassium-rich

molten core. Thus, rocks in Hawaii, known to have poured out as magma less than 200 years ago, have a false potassium-argon dating of 22 million years.

This is exaggerated, say mainstream geologists. In any case, if there is any doubt about one dating method, there are another thirty-nine techniques that are often used for verification. Cross-checking is a normal procedure. Dr. Wiens explains, "The fact that dating methods most often agree with each other is why scientists tend to trust them in the first place."[7]

4. OTHER "CLOCK" PROBLEMS

Dr. Wiens cites other young-earth challenges and gives answers (in parentheses):

❖ Decay rates are poorly known. (By only 2 percent on average, the highest being 5 percent, but this is negligible in dating.)

❖ Decay rates might be slowing down, leading to incorrect old dates. (It cannot be ruled out, but there is no evidence of this. Anyway, all the half-lives of all elements would have had to slow at exactly the same rate, and this is expecting too much.)

❖ Nobody has measured decay rates directly; we only know them by inference. (In the last fifty to eighty years, they have been monitored and shown no change.) Young Earthers would say this is too short a time, especially as some half-lives are recorded in millions of years.

❖ Only atheists and liberals are involved in dating. (There
are many Bible-believing Christians who are involved in
radiometric dating and who can see its validity firsthand.
Most of the members of the Affiliation of Christian
Geologists, in the U.S., are firmly convinced that radiometric dating shows evidence that God created the earth
billions, not thousands, of years ago.)

5. Carbon dating

Carbon-14 is used only for what was once living matter, and
because of its short half-life of 5,730 years, it is not much use
beyond 50,000 years. However, it is worth noting because Young
Earthers insist that it reveals further assumptions or beliefs in science, which may not be
accurate. Carbon-14 is created as cosmic rays—high-energy subatomic particles from outer
space—collide with nitrogen gas in the earth's atmosphere.
Carbon-14 is then absorbed continuously by all living organisms
in the form of carbon dioxide. After the organism dies and
becomes a fossil, the unstable carbon-14 begins to decay. A
piece of the fossil can be burned to convert it into carbon dioxide gas, and a radiation counter detects the electrons given off.

> Carbon-14 is used
> only for what was
> once living matter,
> and because of its
> short half-life of
> 5,730 years, it is not
> much use beyond
> 50,000 years.

The level of carbon-14 in this is compared to the more stable carbon-12 to detect how much radiocarbon has been lost.

Collins Dictionary of Geology gives us our first objective warning about carbon-14: "Several sources of error are introduced into this method, such as the inconstant supply of carbon-14." To be fair, the dictionary does state that, in spite of this, carbon-14 dating has "proved enormously useful." Mainstream geology also has confidence in this dating method. Young Earthers believe that their trust is misplaced for two reasons:

1. The greenhouse model. Formation of carbon-14 must have been greatly affected by what caused the worldwide warm climate. Literally, the earth had the closed and controlled system almost like that of a greenhouse, which explains the lush, verdant fossil record of the Arctic and Antarctic and found in notable excavations in east Greenland. Old Earthers would say that warm climates happened in several geologic ages in both the Mesozoic and Cenozoic eras. Young Earthers are happy with just one period—before Noah's deluge (Genesis 7:11 is read in the light of Genesis 1:2–10—the waters divided above and below).

Young Earthers call on scientific support from scientists like Serge A. Korff, the discoverer and leading expert on cosmic radiation.[8] His work suggested that "when the earth was warmer the atmosphere contained much more water vapor." If, then, the Bible and Korff are right and there was a vapor canopy, the amount of cosmic radiation reaching the earth would have been greatly reduced, and so, too, would the formation of carbon-14. This would result in "considerable overestimates of age," adds Professor Gower, showing a young earth.

2. Fluctuations of carbon-14. Creationists claim that other influences have harmed the formation of carbon-14, such as the heavy carbon dioxide effects of the Industrial Revolution. If ordinary carbon dioxide is not constant in the atmosphere, as in the time of that revolution, it could change the carbon dioxide content.

Old Earthers would insist that carbon-14 has been checked favorably against tree-growth ring dating, as far back as 10,000 years. Also, the technique is supported by ice cores in Greenland and Antarctica, in which each winter's carbon deposits are layered. These go back 100,000 years.[9]

NOTES:

1. Quoted by Ronald L. Numbers, *The Creationists* (Knopf, 1992), 134.

2. Professor D. B. Gower, Pamphlet 207 (Creation Science Movement, 1987).

3. Dr. Roger C. Wiens, "Radiometric Dating: A Christian Perspective," Web site: asa3.org/ASA/resources/Wiens.

4. An isochron diagram, according to *Collins Dictionary of Geology,* is "a diagram in which the relative proportions of radioactive parent and daughter isotopes are plotted against the proportion of the stable isotope (which will not have changed in abundance since the formation of the rock). The increase in the ratio of radiogenic daughter isotope to stable isotope depends on the initial ratio of radioactive parent to stable isotope, and on the age of the specimen. The isotopic rations of minerals from the same rock should be on a straight line (a mineral isochron), the slope of which is proportional to the age."

5. Paul Garner, *On the Rocks: Evolution and the Age of the Earth,* audio tape, Creation Science Movement. The isochron dating he is quoting involves the rubidium-strontium dating method, and the dots in my quotation stand for this. Also given are the examples of contradictions between isochron diagrams.

6. Pamphlet 207.

7. As note 3, p. 17.

8. Serge A. Korff, "Effects of the Cosmic Radiation on Terrestrial Isotope Distribution," *Transactions,* American Geophysical Union 35 (Feb. 1954): 105. Quoted in Whitcomb and Morris, *The Genesis Flood* (Baker, 1961), 375.

9. As note 3, 15–17.

Chapter 6

Recapitulation

Charles Darwin used this chapter title in his *On the Origin of Species* when he was ready for a mini-tour of his argument's strengths and weaknesses. In the midst of the conflicts, we likewise summarize our position. The Old Earth/Young Earth battle lines are now complete. For you and me, it's D-Day.

The creationists are on the march. The battle zones are now global. The secular and religious do battle. Believers of a recent creation and those who want it in the remote and distant past have stopped speaking to each other, if they ever started. The atheists want the "creation" word banned from the language, and still others sit on the fence of unknown time.

Old Earthers have long ago won the propaganda war with

their arguments, and our culture and generation talk in terms of millions of years with the greatest of ease. It goes unquestioned by television, radio, films, newspapers, and magazines. It is as much a fact as the air we breathe. But is it polluted? Is it pure? Is it right? Just before making a final decision, consider two more issues that must be added for completeness and fairness.

THINKING IN CIRCLES?

We noted that Hutton and Lyell identified strata by the fossils they contained. This told them the age of the strata. But how did they know how old the fossils were? Well, they could find this out by the age of the rock strata in which they were found. This surely sounds like circular reasoning.

Geologists acknowledge that this is a problem, but insist that, with the necessary cross-checks and care, it is not a significant one. This is especially true today with the forty radiometric dating methods on which to rely. The *Encyclopedia Britannica* is not convinced:

> It cannot be denied that from a strictly philosophical standpoint geologists are arguing in a circle. The succession of organisms has been determined by a study of their remains embedded in the rocks, and the relative age of the rocks is determined by the organisms that they contain.[1]

Tom Kemp of Oxford wrote in the *New Scientist:*

> A circular argument arises: Interpret the fossil
> record in terms of a particular theory of evo-
> lution, inspect the interpretation, and note that
> it confirms the theory. Well, it would,
> wouldn't it?[2]

Underlining this problem, David M. Raup, Professor of
Geology at the University of Chicago, offers:

> The charge that the construction of the geologic
> scale involves circularity has a certain amount
> of validity. ... Thus,
> the procedure is far
> from ideal and the
> geologic ranges are
> constantly being
> revised (usually
> extended) as new
> occurrences are found.[3]

This circular reasoning
argument is given here for the
sake of completeness and
because Young Earthers set
great store by it. Mainstream
geologists today insist that dating can be achieved without
even bothering with a fossil; their other techniques of dating are
foolproof.

The geological column doesn't exist. In fact, without the theory of evolution, it could not even exist in our minds.

THINKING IN COLUMNS

Remember the geological column? We had problems with it in the Grand Canyon, for example, because a billion years of strata were missing. How was the column dated and made up? Initially, by looking at the fossil record. The whole geological column started off from circular reasoning.

Of course, the solution would be to go and examine the geological column. But we can't. It doesn't exist. In fact, without the theory of evolution, it could not even exist in our minds. This is how the magazine *Geology* explained it:

> A rock that had an early form of an organism was clearly older than the rocks containing later forms. Furthermore, all rocks that had the early form, no matter how far apart those rocks were geographically, would have to be the same age ... fossil successions made it possible to say that the Cambrian rocks are older than the Ordovician rocks. In this way our geologic timetable came into being. ... Without the theory of evolution and the interdisciplinary science of paleontology, it could not exist.[4]

> The rocks, far from forming slowly, cry out "catastrophe."

Returning to the *Encyclopedia Britannica*, we read: "The

end product of the correlation is a mental abstraction called the geological column."[5]

Geology provides a telling comment:

> If a pile were to be made by using the greatest thickness of sedimentary beds of each geological age, it would be at least 100 miles high. … It is, of course, impossible to have even a fraction of this great pile available at any one place. The Grand Canyon of the Colorado, for example, is only one mile deep.[6]

Derek Ager, who wrote *The New Catastrophism,* believes that the rocks, far from forming slowly, cry out "catastrophe." He says of the column, "Nowhere in the world is the record, or even part of it, anywhere near complete."[7]

MOVING ON

The evolution (or otherwise) of earth gives way to the evolution (or otherwise) of life. As we move on, we need to ask the question: Which came first? And would one have been fit enough to survive without the other?

Certainly, Hutton's slow, uniform development of the earth had won some minds in the two generations before Charles Darwin set sail on HMS Beagle out of Devonport in December 1831. And even as the Beagle disappeared over the horizon, Lyell's "bible" on geology was hot off the presses. It was a bestseller long before Darwin's return three years later and had long tolled the death knell of catastrophism by the time Darwin gathered his courage to publish *On the Origin of Species* in 1859.

The truth, probably, is that neither evolution of life nor old-earth ideas would have survived on their own. Both in tandem were needed to pull humanity into modernity and away from the old ideas of a Creator who had made living creatures "after their kind" some six to eight thousand years before.

Hutton and Lyell provided Darwin with time for his evolution. Darwin put purpose into the ages produced by Hutton and Lyell.

Have we swapped one myth for another?

Whatever, the old Creator story was now firmly classified as myth— merely a useful model that might not be true but enshrined uplifting, guiding ideas and ideals for humanity. Myth fell before the might of Darwin's well-woven theory. And here is a question at the heart of our book. Have we swapped one myth for another? Is our twenty-first-century culture on a firm base?

One thought has been expressed in various forms in recent times. Is the last of modernity's three great thinkers about to topple? The twentieth century was founded on Marx, Freud, and Darwin. Marxism fragmented as the Berlin Wall fell. Freud lost his number one rating, criticized for his obsession with sex and childhood, and his failure to understand women.[8] As I write, a new twenty-volume translation of his works comes off the presses, trying to revive his reputation.

Darwin is the only one left standing, and his theory is in crisis. Let's see what state it's really in.

NOTES:

1. R. H. Rastal, *Encyclopedia Britannica,* vol. X, 1985, 168.

2. Tom Kemp, *New Scientist* 108 (Dec. 5, 1985): 67.

3. David Raup, *Field Museum of Natural History Bulletin* 54 (March 1983): 21.

4. Putman and Bassett, *Geology,* 544.

5. *Encyclopedia Britannica,* vol. X, 1985, 779.

6. Von Engeln and Caster, *Geology,* 1985, 417.

7. Derek Ager, *The New Catastrophism* (Cambridge University Press, 1993), 14.

8. Brett Kahr, *Complete Works of Sigmund Freud* (Penguin Press, 2002).

❖ EVOLUTION OF LIFE

Chapter 7

Evolution

Our chapter heading must rank as one of the most abused words in the English dictionary.

To a dwindling few, it is pure Darwin à la *Origins*—species originating through unhurried and gradual change as nature selects the fittest and weeds out the weakest links in the survival game called life.

To the majority in the twenty-first century, it is Darwin updated (neo-Darwinism)—*On the Origin of Species* plus or minus a range of new hypotheses and theories. It embraces the exciting discoveries and developments of biology in miniature, at the molecular level. It also includes a fresh controversy. Does evolution slide gradually from one species to another, or is it more like a game of hopscotch, with short jumps every now and then?

To the majority of Christians in Britain, it is the way God has chosen to bring about His creation. The fingers of deity, more or less, urge and guide. Some want to include God for the "difficult bits." Some see Him rather as a fountain from which all of life and evolution flow. Others prefer the idea of God as the ground of all being.

To the minority of Christians, evolution is the biggest con job ever pulled on mankind. Of these, a section say that humanity will believe anything to escape the need of God. Others discern spiritual warfare, conspiracy, and the devil.

> Evolution is the biggest con job ever pulled on mankind.... humanity will believe anything to escape the need of God.

To radical, free-thinking scientists like Australia's Dr. Michael Denton, evolution is a theory in crisis. It is neo-Darwinism plus the still-as-yet Unknown. These lone, latter-day Galileos fret about the many unexplained gaps in the theory. Galileo, when faced with a faulty theory of the heavens going round the earth, worried over it until his sun-centered plan emerged. Likewise, evolution's radicals ravage and gnaw at Darwin's leftovers, searching for a breakthrough. They are certain that something is missing at the heart of Darwin's system. The other option for them is impossible to contemplate: a return to the old Creator idea. When radicals write their critical papers or books, their first paragraph or chapter inevitably disowns Genesis and especially "those fundamentalist creationists." With that, they journey on into the unknown, searching for the missing key that will finally unlock the mystery of where we've come from and why we are like we are.

One final group uses evolution as its main work tool. If it exists, then it evolves. That's the motto that drives the -ology professionals. Psychologists, sociologists, anthropologists, biologists, and so on find criticism of evolution particularly hard to bear. They have so much to lose, so much to rewrite if it all crumbles to nothing.

> Psychologists, sociologists, anthropologists, biologists, and so on find criticism of evolution particularly hard to bear. They have so much to lose, so much to rewrite if it all crumbles to nothing.

DEFINITIONS

Whenever I use "evolution" in this book, I am adopting the encyclopedia Encarta's safe and general definition. It is "the complex of processes by which living organisms originated on earth and have been diversified through sustained changes in form and function."

> A species that invents a new flavor of itself is undergoing straightforward variation. The only time it becomes controversial is when it is used as evidence for macro-evolution.

And, while on definitions, a qualification: the terms "evolutionist" and "creationist" are often used as frontline insults traded across the no-man's land of our battle zone. Here, they are simply handy, neutral descriptions. The creationist is, no more and no less, a believer in a young earth/universe made in a literal six-day working week. The evolutionist is one who accepts the above Encarta definition and gives chance the credit for change. For those evolutionists who credit a Creator, the term "theistic evolutionist" is used.

LITTLE AND LARGE

Back to biology. Most break evolution down into "mini-" or "maxi-." Others use "micro-" or "macro-evolution." It means the same thing. The "micro" version is not really evolution at all. It's another misuse of the word. A species that invents a new flavor of itself is undergoing straightforward variation. This even the most fundamental of creationists applauds. Of course,

there is variation within species. The only time it becomes controversial is when it is used as evidence for macro-evolution.
This is where the real battle begins for the creationist.

Micro-evolution, or variation, can be illustrated with the aid
of my beautiful assistant, Lady, the family mongrel. She is as
unlike her wolf-based origins as she could possibly be; more a
delicate golden Heinz-57 cross between labrador, lurcher, and
whippet with a fox face. As such, she is living proof that so-
called micro-evolution, or variation, happens.

Charles Darwin saw this in the wild as well as in domesticated animals. Birds, caterpillars, and moths all boasted
rich varieties. If they could change in small ways before his
eyes over a few generations, then why not in big ways over
many generations? It seemed so obvious. Darwin's
Galapagos finches, for example, changed to cope with
harder or softer food supplies on the islands where groups
of them became isolated. It led to the same species diversi-
fying, growing different sizes and shapes of beaks to cope
with different menus on different islands. Natural selection
gave the advantage to those with the right-for-the-job beaks.
The fitter-beaked birds survived better and so bred to pass
on their advantage to successive generations. Darwin reasoned that, given competition from other species plus
changing habitats and a few million years, a struggling
species would eventually turn into a sleeker survival
machine, and even another species. It was plausible. It
seemed so right. Surely, given the existence of simple life
forms, there was no reason why natural pressures should not
create the countless varieties that surround us.

And not only creatures in the wild. Take domesticated

animals, urged Darwin. They were bred to favor certain beneficial traits—the racing pigeon, the thoroughbred horse, the
working dog. Steve Jones in *Almost Like a Whale*, his rewrite
of *Origins*, states,

> Variation within existing forms can, with
> human help, bring forth new kinds of creatures
> quite different from their ancestors. Evolution
> on the farm is a small-scale version of that in
> Nature. ... It shows that species are not set in
> stone, but are always in flux. ... Variation under
> domestication—in fields, zoos and in living-
> rooms—is still powerful evidence for his
> [Darwin's] theory.[1]

SOME PROBLEMS

Steve Jones puts the strength of evolution in a persuasive, readable manner. He stresses the inevitability of change in life, in the
face of natural selection and in a struggle for existence, explaining that it would have been a most extraordinary fact if variations had not occurred that were useful to each being's welfare.[2]

True, he acknowledges, our "ignorance of the laws of variation is profound." In less than one case out of a hundred "can
we pretend to assign any reason why this or that part differs,
more or less, from the same part in the parents. But in those rare
cases where reasons can be seen, the same laws of variation are
always found to apply."[3]

Darwin, and Jones the modernizer, are confident of their
theory in their respective books, though they each devote a

whole chapter to the difficulties of their theory. "Many of them are very grave," according to Steve Jones.[4] It is mostly these that have bothered the creationists and led to their fight back:

- ❖ The absence or rarity of transitional links between various groups of creatures.

- ❖ The sterile fate of hybrids. Once changed, impotent creatures cannot pass on their variations.

- ❖ The seeming impossibility of creatures changing habitats, from water to land and from land to air, and even from land back to water, to produce whales, dolphins, and so on.

- ❖ The problems of natural selection producing complex organs such as the eye.

- ❖ The hidden turmoil in our genes demands more than natural selection to make evolution work.

Some of the biggest evolutionary headaches come from the "rebels" of the animal kingdom, those who fail to follow the lifestyles of their parents, for "such moves could not, it seems, be achieved by gradual change, as there must be a shift in the dozens of characters that separate the old version from the new," says Jones. He explains:

> To imagine from the behavior of an eccentric bear that a whole race could, in time, be rendered more and more aquatic, till at last a beast was produced as monstrous as a whale, is a little much to ask even of natural selection.[5]

At one level, evolution looks plausible, especially in the micro variation. Four-foot-tall great Danes and four-inch-high chihuahuas we can cope with. Bears turning into whales is a little harder. Perhaps peering a little deeper down a microscope will help. Just how does it—micro or macro—all work?

NOTES:

1. Steve Jones, *Almost Like a Whale* (Anchor, 2000), 32–33.

2. Ibid., 130–131.

3. Ibid., 154.

4. Ibid., 186.

5. Ibid., 164.

Chapter 8

Evolution in Action

M icroscopes adorned the desks of gentlemen scientists by the nineteenth century, but lack of power and a limited knowledge were handicaps. It meant that Charles Darwin mainly used his eyes to detect change in nature. He observed the wild and tame at home and abroad and saw "micro" changes. He then, nervously and mustering great courage, took the massive leap of extending the changes beyond the species to the macro level of evolution—all crafted by natural selection, the survival of the fittest.

Now, with multilense and stereoscopic microscopes, the electron micrograph, X-ray crystallography, and the like, we marvel at a beautiful panorama of biology in miniature. Today, we are at home with proteins that have to be magnified a million times before we can see them. Large 3-D models of the very basis of life—DNA, deoxyribonucleic acid—decorate laboratory alcoves. At the time we were conquering Everest, Francis Crick, Maurice Wilkins, and James Dewey Watson were introducing us to their "double helix" miracle molecule. Slowly, the laws and patterns of heredity and natural selection began to be laid bare.

The city-like layout of a living cell awaited exploration. It has its "town hall," housing the blueprints for the whole metropolis—the nucleus of the cell, with its DNA wrapped in a double helix shape in chromosomes, on the "arms" of which are located the genetic codes of life. Everything runs from this bustling headquarters.

The "water authority" is controlled, keeping everything floating in about 65 percent of liquid suitable for vital biochemical reactions. "Public and race relations" ensures cooperation among the population, workforce, and departments using enzyme proteins to promote good chemical reactions between all concerned. "Emigration and migration" (plus sewage) controls a network of pumps, channels, and sluice gates, selectively admitting minerals and nutrients and excreting waste products. "Construction and maintenance" looks after the shape and size with the cytoskeleton. These departments also oversee the district offices, power stations, and direct works "factories" (the proteins) that produce all that is needed and make the whole place function.

A strategic "transport authority" is vital. The DNA blueprint is constantly unwinding its double helix, copying off from itself work schedules for city departments. Waves of messengers (RNA—ribonucleic acids) are then sent to the thousands of protein work sites. Each work site is its own translation unit (ribosome) because all messages arrive encoded.

As with any "town hall," changes happen from term to term. A slight mutation in politics and policy can produce a different outcome. In the cell, a slight defect in one blood gene can cause the whole cytoskeleton to cave in, turning a normal round cell into the doughnut of sickle-cell anemia. But a mix of genes can also bring advantage to an offspring that helps it survive in time of warfare and shortage. These can then go on to produce others, some of which will have more advantageous gene mixes, and so the survival of the fittest goes on.

This, minus a thousand and one other "city-like" functions, is one of our cells. It is sufficient to remind us of how slight changes in miniature can bring changes at species level. However, this level also is not without difficulties.

MORE PROBLEMS

How did such a complex cell evolve? This, for the creationist, is the first question. It's not a problem for the theistic evolutionists, with God underwriting everything, but it is an ongoing headache for the evolutionist who relies on chance.

It is easy to see how a village evolves into a city, but how did dead, inorganic something become a living, breathing self-supporting organism that could then go on to reproduce itself? Evolutionists have tried many solutions:

❖ Elementary life forms originating in hot undersea geysers.

❖ Crystals gradually evolving into greater and greater complexity.

❖ The primeval soup theory: a stagnant pond of chemicals sparked into life by lightning. Harold Urey and Stanley Miller reproduced what they believed to be early earth conditions in a vacuum and bombarded it with electricity. They later found traces of amino acids, the building blocks of proteins, as well as some compounds found in living cells. The Miller-Urey experiment was finally shelved after it was revealed that an early earth atmosphere couldn't possibly have matched their starting position. Their concoction was a nonstarter.[1]

❖ The seed of life delivered to a young earth by comets, meteorites, or interplanetary dust. Scientists at

> "The complexity of the simplest known type of cell is so great that it is impossible to accept that such an object could have been thrown together suddenly by some kind of freakish, vastly improbable, event. Such an occurrence would be indistinguishable from a miracle."

NASA claim to have created "primitive cells"—empty membranes that could have protected the seed of life en route to planet earth.[2]

All these are brave and serious scientific attempts. The reason why the search for life's origins has moved to outer space is the difficulty of solving the problem on planet earth. The twenty-first-century rush to reexamine Mars for signs of life, plus the Seti program, ever listening for intelligent radio waves from other galaxies, is part of the drive to reinforce the evolutionists' belief that life is automatic once a planet has the required elements. Unfortunately for them, life is not so simple.

The main enigma of life's origins is the minimum requirements for the simplest self-replicating cell. Harold Morowitz, an American biochemist, once worked out that a cell needed the following:

❖ A membrane (a minimum of five proteins would be needed to build the walls with necessary fats).

❖ An energy power pack (at least eight proteins needed).

❖ A simple DNA sequence (at least 100,000 nucleotides long) plus a way of building new DNA (ten more proteins).[3]

❖ Protein-making apparatus plus translation units (ribosomes) and the necessary messenger RNA (at least eighty proteins).

Morowitz explained, "This is the smallest hypothetical cell that we can envisage within the context of current biochemical thinking. It is almost certainly a lower limit, since we have allowed no control functions, no vitamin metabolism and extremely limited intermediary metabolism. Such a cell would be very vulnerable to environmental fluctuation."[4]

Australian molecular biologist Dr. Michael Denton commented, "The complexity of the simplest known type of cell is so great that it is impossible to accept that such an object could have been thrown together suddenly by some kind of freakish, vastly improbable, event. Such an occurrence would be indistinguishable from a miracle."[5]

These problems are not aired by creationists. All these come from radical scientists trying to discover the meaning of life and how it has arrived here and now. However, the difficulties have been an encouragement to creationists, and they have helped them to stop retreating. We now see how they have arrived at their new and challenging position in society.

NOTES:

1. The Urey-Miller experiment is highlighted in Jonathan Wells, *The Icons of Evolution,* Regnery Publishing, 2000. Wells outlines a dozen supports of evolution that have fallen into disrepute.

2. www.bbcnewsonline, 29 January 2001.

3. DNA is made up of a string of compounds called nucleotides. Imagine a ladder shaped like a helter-skelter. The sides are made up of sugars and a phosphate group. Each rung of the "helter-skelter" ladder has two of the four nucleotides that occur in DNA. These are adenine (A), guanine (G), cytosine (C), and thymine (T). A attached to one strand will tend to pair up with T, while G is happier associating with C. In between, in the middle of the "rung," is a hydrogen bond, a chemical interaction. A, G, C, and T are sequenced to form coded messages—genes. When DNA unwraps itself briefly, it is copied into amino acids, the messenger RNA that goes on a marathon to instruct the relevant "factory" protein to do its job.

4. H. J. Morowitz, *The Minimum Size of Cells,* 1966. Quoted in Dr. Michael Denton, *Evolution: A Theory in Crisis* (Alder & Alder, 1985), 263.

5. Denton, *Evolution: A Theory in Crisis* (Alder & Alder, 1985), 264.

Chapter 9

How We Got Here

The creationist revival has been a journey of colorful characters, literature, honest internal warfare, and society splits. The recent controversy is but the latest stop on a well-traveled road. The outstanding milestones lining the path from creationist obscurity are definitely the books and their authors. I have left out many dealing with theistic evolution, such as the influential Derek Kidner commentary on Genesis, and booklets and books by Dr. Victor Pearce, plus many others. These are referred to later. In the creationists' battle, the pen's might is beyond doubt.

OMPHALUS

We travel back to the nineteenth century to Christian writers contending with fossils and uniformitarianism. Henry Gosse, for example, published *Omphalus* in 1857, two years before Darwin's Origins. He proclaimed that the biblical Adam had been made complete with navel (omphalus) even though he didn't have a mother, and that God had likewise created a fully mature universe complete with full modern conveniences.

We could dawdle in these early days and, for example, spend profitable time at the Victoria Institute, set up to maintain biblical purity following Darwin's *On the Origin of Species*. In its heyday, its membership included fellows of the Royal Society. We could join the Acworth Circle and the Evolutionary Protestant Movement in the early twentieth century and write a learned tome on the colorful characters, splits, and consequent new societies that emerged, but this has already been done well by Ronald L. Numbers.[1]

Our starting point must be the modern revival of the creation/evolution debate with the publication of ...

THE GENESIS FLOOD (1961)

Its two authors set out to present the biblical record (John C. Whitcomb, Jr.) alongside a new interpretation of old catastrophism, and in particular a worldwide deluge (Henry M. Morris). The introduction in my 1979 copy (even by then in its twenty-third reprinting) states:

> Frankly recognizing the inadequacies of uniformitarianism and evolutionism as unifying principles, the authors propose a biblically-based system of creationism and catastrophism ... the

uniformist approach to the study of the earth
has proved unable to explain many of the most
important physical structures and phenomena.
… The publishers believe that The Genesis
Flood will prove to be one of the most widely
discussed and possibly one of the most significant books of our times.

They were right. This 512-page scholarly treatment allowed
creationists to walk tall across the world. The amazing growth in
Britain can be traced to this one volume. In New Zealand, TGF, as
the book is affectionately tagged, was credited with converting 27
percent of the population to creationism. Worldwide, creationists
were still treated as quaint and amusing, but now they could bear
it and even feel sorry for those not in the know. Archaeological
discoveries in the Near East were also winning new respect for the
Scriptures, and many a fundamentalist had the Bible under one
arm while snuggling TGF under the other.

EVOLUTION OR CREATION (1967)

Professor H. Enoch's book went into several reprints and editions
and gave a popular scholarly treatment from a zoologist's point
of view. It was written mainly for his university students and, as
such, had ongoing influence over a generation. Writing his own
testimony (quaintly in the third person), Professor Enoch stated:

This critical study of the subject has driven him
to the conclusion that the theory of evolution is
not established fact, and there is no definite

proof that animals and plants have come to
their present stage through such a process
rather than by creation as stated in the Bible.
This conviction has been further established by
the accumulation of scientific facts that have
come to light since.

THE GREAT BRAIN ROBBERY (1975)

This was a pocket paperback in which David C. C. Watson gave
British readers a brief tour of TGF's main selling points. More
than this, it had the seal of approval of one of the great orators
of the day, Dr. Martyn Lloyd-Jones. Watson wrote:

> £2m of the notes lost in the Great Train
> Robbery may never be recovered. But spiritual
> and intellectual riches, though lost to one gen-
> eration, may be recovered by the next. ... The
> present dogmatic teaching of Evolution
> Guesswork as "fact" is closely akin to brain-
> washing, and is indefensible on any logic,
> ethics or democracy.

Watson (not to be confused with the famous preacher without the initials) wrote with much feeling. He claimed at an
industrial tribunal that his stand against evolution had lost him
his teaching post. He didn't persuade the judges, but many in
British creationism gave him support.

Many more books and films from this golden decade could
be mentioned, including *The World That Perished* and *Origin of*

the Solar System, both by J. C. Whitcomb, *Darwin, Evolution and Creation* by Paul Zimmerman, and *Radio-Carbon Dating* by Dr. A. J. Monty White. All had influence.

THE SELFISH GENE (1979)

Amazingly, leading atheist Richard Dawkins, and similar media scientists, may have been an inspiration to creationists. A reaction set in against Professor Dawkins's reduction of humans to "nothing more than ... throwaway survival machines" for genes. His militant atheism, often dismissive of and offensive to Christians, caused the very thing he sought to eliminate—a creationist revival. Some Christians, seeing Dawkins use evolution to justify his atheism, therefore voted against evolution. It was, and is, a very strong gut emotion, compounded by the liberal wing of the church in the 1960s and 1970s increasingly reassigning early Genesis and other large chunks of Scripture to myth. Conservative evangelicals' reaction was to stand against liberal and atheist alike as People of the Book. Also, they wanted to underline the Fall (of Genesis 3) as the time when death entered into the world and consequently rejected the survival-of-the-fittest, dinosaur-kill-dinosaur evolution.

HEN'S TEETH AND HORSE'S TOES (1983)

This, and many other papers and books by the late Harvard Professor of Geology and paleontology Stephen Jay Gould (plus colleague Niles Eldredge), unwittingly inspired creationism across the world. Creationists used (and sometimes abused) the claims of Gould and Eldredge that the fossil record did not support the gradual evolution proposed by Darwin.

> The single greatest problem that the fossil record posed for Darwinism was the Cambrian explosion of around 600 million years ago. Nearly all the animal phyla appeared in the rocks of this period, without a trace of the evolutionary ancestors that Darwinists required.

Gould said that the single greatest problem that the fossil record posed for Darwinism was the Cambrian explosion of around 600 million years ago. Nearly all the animal phyla appeared in the rocks of this period, without a trace of the evolutionary ancestors that Darwinists required. He added, "All paleontologists know that the fossil record contains precious little in the way of intermediate forms; transitions between major groups are characteristically abrupt."[2]

Creationists couldn't contain themselves and sometimes, rather naughtily, used his quotes out of context. What he and Eldredge were at pains to point out was that Darwinian evolution was wrong only in that it insisted on gradual change. Gould and Eldredge instead proposed a hopscotch progression. Species, they maintained, were stable (in equilibria) for huge periods, but these were punctuated by short bursts of sudden change—hence the shortage of fossils. They christened it "punctuated equilibria." Some creationists used the quotes without mentioning this, causing both Gould and Eldredge embarrassment in their disciplines.

The quotes used in this section come from The Revised Quote Book, published by Australia's Creation Science Foundation, who at least acknowledge "that the vast majority of authorities quoted are themselves ardent believers in evolution."

Punctuated equilibria came under heavy fire from Darwinists, who insisted that if evolution was to rely on sudden "hopeful monsters" appearing, it might as well throw in its lot with magicians or a Creator. Creationists were quick to agree with the Creator idea. Other favorite quotes from Gould included:

> The extreme rarity of transitional forms in the fossil record persists as the trade secret of paleontology. The evolutionary trees that adorn our textbooks have data only at the tips and nodes of their branches; the rest is inference, however reasonable, not the evidence of fossils. ... paleontologists have paid an exorbitant price for Darwin's argument.[3]

> Paleontologists (and evolutionary biologists in general) are famous for their facility in devising plausible stories; but they often forget that plausible stories need not be true.[4]

The essence of Darwin lies in a single phrase:
natural selection is the creative force of evolutionary change. No one denies that natural
selection will play a negative role in eliminat-
ing the unfit. Darwinian theories require that it
create the fit as well.[5]

EVOLUTION: A THEORY IN CRISIS (1986)

This had enormous impact among creationists in the U.S.,
Britain, and Australia. For the first time, here was a non-
Christian scholar rejecting Darwin's evolution as it was tradi-
tionally understood. *The Spectator* reviewer said of Dr. Michael
Denton's book, "What will be most embarrassing to the neo-
Darwinians ... will be Denton's revelation that the evidence
from his speciality, molecular biology, lends them no support."
Publishers Adler & Adler introduced their prize publication
with the following comment:

> This authoritative and remarkably accessible
> book by a molecular biologist shows how rap-
> idly accumulating evidence is threatening the
> basic assumptions of orthodox Darwinism.
> Although the theory appears to be correct
> regarding the emergence of new species, its
> larger claims to account for the relationship
> between classes and orders, let alone the origin
> of life, appear to be based on shaky foundations
> at best. Not only has paleontology failed to
> come up with the fossil "missing links" that

Darwin anticipated, but the hypothetical recon-
structions of major evolutionary developments—
such as linking birds to reptiles—are beginning
to look more like fantasies than serious conjec-
tures. ... At a fundamental level of molecular
structure, each member of a class seems equally
representative of that class, and no species
appear to be in any real sense "intermediate"
between two classes. Nature, in sum, appears to
be profoundly discontinuous.

DARWIN ON TRIAL (1991)

"Unquestionably the best critique of Darwinism I have ever
read ... it will prove a severe embarrassment to the Darwinian
establishment." So wrote Dr. Michael Denton.[6]

Professor Philip E. Johnson was the author who put the
standard evolution theory on trial. He was eminently qualified
for the task as a Berkeley University professor of law, special-
izing in the logic of arguments. His evolution critics said that,
like all lawyers, Johnson chose his arguments carefully, leaving
out anything that didn't suit his case.

This book was bought in bulk by creationists, although
ironically the book was as much a lesson for them as the atheistic evolutionists. Johnson disliked anybody using science to
support a cause. It always turned such people into fanatics. He
added, "The debate about evolution has all too often pitted religious fundamentalists against science, the Bible against empir-
ical observation. This antagonism springs from the creed of
Darwinism."

DARWIN'S BLACK BOX (1996)

Michael J. Behe, Professor of Biochemistry at Lehigh University, Pennsylvania, did what nobody had done before. He set forth the biochemical challenge to evolution. "No one can propose to defend Darwin," commented critic David Berlinski, author of *A Tour of Calculus,* "without meeting the challenges set out in this superbly written and compelling book."

At its most simple, Behe states that there are too many complex "mousetraps" in chemistry and molecular biology. A "mousetrap," he explains, is an "irreducible complexity."

> Science has no adequate explanations of how these systems could have evolved, despite much research.

Reduce the mousetrap in any way, or alter its parts, and it becomes useless. To be a mousetrap, the complexity has to have all its parts present, and it needs to have them from the very beginning.

He tells his readers that there are many similar irreducible complexities in biology, such as the defense mechanism of the body, the blood supply, and the clotting mechanism. Science, he writes, has no adequate explanations of how these systems could have evolved, despite much research. He maintains that because the complexities are irreducible, science will never be able to explain them. He prefers to think of it as evidence for intelligent design in the universe.

Behe would not put himself in the creationist camp, but nevertheless this has not stopped creationists claiming his book and arguments for their own case. Professor Behe accepts an ancient universe and is at present content with the idea of common descent (all organisms sharing a common ancestor). However, he writes that he cannot find evidence for it at the very foundation of life, and he thinks his present beliefs may themselves evolve with new advances in the science of the tiny.

> The cumulative results show with piercing clarity that life is based on machines—machines made of molecules! Molecular machines haul cargo from one place in the cell to another among "highways" made of other molecules, while still others act as cables, ropes, and pulleys to hold the cell in shape. ...
>
> Thus the details of life are finely calibrated, and the machinery of life is enormously complex. ...
>
> The complexity of life's foundations has paralyzed science's attempt to account for it; molecular machines raise an as-yet-impenetrable barrier to Darwin's universal reach. ...
>
> Although Darwin's mechanism—natural selection working on variation—might explain many things, however, I do not believe it explains molecular life. I also do not think it surprising that the new science of the very small might change the way we view the less small.[7]

I have been very selective in my choice of books and characters, and I hasten to stress that these are only milestones along the journey. It gives you, the reader, a quick tour of the revival in creationism. It also equips you with enough information to travel whichever legs of the journey you personally find interesting.

Now we must deal with the real issues of evolution and creation, and first we look at one that has already intrigued—the fossil record.

NOTES:

1. Ronald L. Numbers, *The Creationists—The Evolution of Scientific Creationism* (Knopf, 1992).

2. Stephen Jay Gould, "The Return of Hopeful Monsters," *Natural History,* vol. LXXXVI (6), (June/July 1977): 24.

3. "Evolution's Erratic Pace," *Natural History,* vol. LXXXVI (May 1977): 14.

4. "The Shape of Evolution: a comparison of real and random clades," *Paleobiology,* vol. 3(1) (1977): 34–45.

5. As note 3, p. 28.

6. Philip E. Johnson, *Darwin on Trial* (Monarch Publications, 1991) back page.

7. Michael J. Behe, *Darwin's Black Box* (Touchstone, 1996) 6.

Chapter 10

The Fossil Problem

C harles Darwin, like or loathe his theory, was a man of great courage. In 1859, he invited a worldwide change of heart and head, challenging civilization to rewrite the whole of science and religion. He knew he was shaking and stirring the two most cherished realms of human life. He knew that his scientific peers, the press, and the public would mock him. He knew the difficulties that were still unresolved in his theory. Not only this, in his book he had made sure his readers would know the shortcomings of his theory. He had underlined them. To be sure, it was his way of preventing greater ridicule by showing that he had seen them. But he also wanted to ensure that his readers would have the full facts so that they could make their own judgments.

For one thing, the complexity of the eye scared him into

silence. How could such a thing possibly have evolved? And there was an even bigger cause of writer's block, enough to stay his pen for a generation after disembarking from HMS Beagle. His biggest headache was the fossil record, and only fear of somebody beating him to the punch made him finally head for the publishers.

Charles Darwin only resolved his difficulties by appealing to the future. He and his theory were right, he decided. What was wrong was his and nineteenth-century society's poor knowledge. This comes out as he explains himself concerning the missing links in the fossil record of that time.

> Why then is not every geological formation and every stratum full of such intermediate links? Geology assuredly does not reveal any such finely graduated organic chain; and this, perhaps, is the most obvious and serious objection that can be urged against the theory. The explanation lies, as I believe, in the extreme imperfection of the geological record.[1]

The "extreme imperfection of the geological record" must surely now be less imperfect.

A day would come, he proposed, when all the missing links would be laid bare. This idea was to inspire the greatest ever treasure hunt on the planet. Ever since, it has been dug up, plowed, and sifted by six generations of avid hunters. When they weren't scouring the earth, its crust was being mined or excavated by commerce or catastrophe—flood, volcano, earthquake, and even cratered by meteorites.

So, what of the fossil record now? The "extreme imperfection of the geological record" must surely now be less imperfect. Apparently not, according to paleontologists.

> The record of evolution is still surprisingly
> jerky and, ironically, we have even fewer exam-
> ples of evolutionary transitions than we had in
> Darwin's time. By this I mean that some classic
> cases of Darwinian change in the fossil record,
> such as the evolution of the horse in North
> America, have had to be discarded or modified
> as a result of more detailed information.[2]

So wrote Dr. David M. Raup, Curator of Geology at the Field Museum of Natural History in Chicago, in his 1979 article, "Conflicts between Darwin and paleontology."

But that was a generation ago. What of now? In the 2000 rewrite of Darwin's *On the Origin of Species,* Professor Jones is unable to improve.

> The fossil record—in defiance of Darwin's
> whole idea of gradual change—often makes
> great leaps from one form to the next. Far from
> the display of intermediates to be expected
> from slow advance through natural selection,
> many species appear without warning, persist
> in fixed form, and disappear, leaving no

descendants. Geology assuredly does not reveal
any finely graduated organic chain, and this is
the most obvious and gravest objection that can
be urged against the theory of evolution.[3]

No fossil links, so no evolution! That's the creationist equation. End of story. But both Darwin and Jones insist that this equation is wrong, and for the following reasons.

DECAY

Corruption, writes Steve Jones, has five stages—"fresh, bloat, active rot, post-decay and dry remains." Drop down dead during a remote hike at the height of summer, and in only three weeks your clothed skeleton will be found. Years later, just shreds of anorak jacket and your Doc Martins shoes will mark a modest pile of dust. We live amid a billion creatures, yet seldom see a corpse. A few interesting exceptions have been unearthed: the archaeoptery fossil bird, various kinds of elephant, a growing number of dinosaurs, and the remains of our own ancestors.

> If God made the planet 6,000 years ago, why did He make it look so old?

"Any of those bones is conclusive evidence of evolution," writes Steve Jones, "and is in itself enough to demolish the creationist case."

"Not so," a creationist would counter. "The number of inter-mediate and transitional links between all living and extinct species must have been inconceivably great," a creationist could say, quoting Jones's own words back at him.[4] "Almost none are found," Professor Jones adds.

"Almost none" is a rather naughty use of words by Steve Jones, who usually uses language brilliantly in his book. He means "comparatively almost none." This still amounts to millions of fos-sil specimens in thousands of museums across the world. London's Natural History Museum alone has six million examples of marine snail fossils. Finds even include difficult-to-preserve soft-tissue items like skin and jellyfish.[5]

> If nature slowly evolved the creatures, why did it make such a good job of hiding the evidence?

The creationist would challenge Mr. Darwin and Professor Jones thus: Every fossil expert in six generations has dug in thousands of well-preserved fossil "graveyards." Isn't it strange, then, that not one noncontroversial missing fossil link has yet been found? Even the archaeopteryx and other appar-ent links, creationists insist, have now been classified by most experts into known species or classes and are no longer consid-ered intermediary.

The evolutionist, of course, challenges the creationist: if God made the planet 6,000 years ago, why did He make it look so old? The creationist responds with another question: if nature slowly evolved the creatures, why did it make such a good job of hiding the evidence?

Even Richard Dawkins concedes the point about fossils: "It is as though they were just planted there, without any evolutionary history."[6]

LAPSE OF TIME

Darwin and Jones ask us to consider the wonder that anything survived millions of years. Take, for instance, the destructive power of water. Melting, expanding ice can crumble the best-laid roads of man in a matter of years. It can wear away ancient pyramids. Australia is said to be the most "exhausted land," with few mountains, and is in the last stages of decay.

"Some places give the dead a chance," explains Steve Jones, "but others are less kind." Wonder not where all the missing fossils are, suggests the evolutionist. Marvel that any are there at all.

Creationists understand what the elements can do, especially water. They still want to swap "millions" [of years] for "thousands," and we're back to the dating game.

SUDDEN APPEARANCE

Steve Jones states, "The abrupt manner in which whole groups suddenly appear in certain formations has been urged as a fatal objection. … If numerous species, belonging to the same genera or families, did start into life all at once, the fact would be a severe blow to the theory of descent with slow modification." In defense, he cites the archaeopteryx and other finds. He claims that the fossil bird came from a smaller version of the voracious velociraptor (the two-legged terror of *Jurassic Park* film fame). He knows this is a massive jump but suggests the turkey-sized unenlargia as an intermediary. He describes this as a feathered dinosaur with short arms that move the same way as wings.

A Creator making kinds and varieties would, of course, use similar DNA that constructs similar body parts.

The creationist would point out that this is still a "huge gap," and Professor Jones would agree. The creationist would also stress that the presence of similar bodies in fossils is not evidence that one descended from another. It is, they say, a good indication that they were made by the same "Architect" using a well-proven design to produce various forms.

Steve Jones is able to add one extra argument to Darwin's original defense: that of DNA sequencing. The professor says that "lost birds … left footprints in the DNA of their descendants." Today's birds are the products of slowly evolving genes, he states. We can see how DNA changes from one species to another and, assuming they've evolved into one another, we can identify the missing gaps in the sequence and, bingo! find our missing links.

The book's title, *Almost Like a Whale,* comes from this argument. The swimming bear and the whale have related

DNA. In fact, so do we. This DNA version of Happy Families concludes that ape and man are "cousins" because they share 98.5 percent of their genes.

However, the creationist would stick to his architectural argument. A Creator making kinds and varieties would, of course, use similar DNA to construct similar body parts.

The whale, the bear, the bird, the dinosaur, even the unenlargia and humans, all have similar bone structures jutting out of their bodies at similar places. This does not mean we evolved from a common ancestor or each other, says the creationist. This is about a Creator keeping to a winning design formula.

So, what about those now-useless organs our bodies are packed with, the evolutionist would challenge? These vestigial remnants include the vermiform appendix and the coccyx. Don't be too quick to write off these, a creationist would caution. There is evidence that the appendix is used in fetal development, and it would be hard to use the facilities without a good anchor for the posterior muscles. These are not merely leftovers from our alleged cousins.

LIFE'S BIG BANG

According to evolutionary theory, life appears to have suddenly exploded 550 million years ago without any time to change. As Steve Jones himself explains, "Most of the major divisions to today's animal kingdom—the phyla—appear just after the start of the Cambrian. Before then, little is found. If evolution is gradual, how could so many forms spring all at once into existence?"

Is this evidence of sudden appearance without time for selection right? Steve Jones is emphatic: "The answer is, without doubt, no." First, he says, there is evidence that stromatolite limestone mounds, made up of tiny microbes, existed in pre-Cambrian days. But how then did microbes change into the highly developed creatures of the Cambrian strata? Well, says Jones, perhaps DNA went through a "crucial change"—rather like a fruit fly gene can, with the help of genetic scientists, sprout a leg where an antenna should be.

At this point, it seems that Steve Jones has stopped rewriting Darwin's *On the Origin of Species* and started writing his own version of evolution. Darwin's gradualism appears to be out. Now, creatures suddenly start appearing with different body parts in one generation.

No, says Jones—the apparent sudden appearance is not real. It is the geological record that is wrong. "The Cambrian explosion, so called, is a failure of the geological record rather than the Darwinian machine."

Before the Cambrian, animals only had soft tissue that could not be fossilized.

This is a good point. Remember the trilobite, says Jones. Before it got its shell, there would only have been the soft body and that would not have easily fossilized.

The creationist would point out that this is an argument with no evidence. Just silence. You cannot argue from something that isn't there. You cannot just make something up to suit a theory you like for other reasons. And, in any case, they would add, what about the highly developed eye that appears in creatures at the very beginning of the Cambrian period? Creationist Ian Campbell, in his booklet *A Case for Creation,* introduces the nautiloid as "a squid-like animal living in a long straight shell that can be up to nine feet in length, a member of the most complex group of invertebrates that we know anything about—the cephalopod molluscs. It has an eye very similar to the human eye, which as we know is complex almost beyond belief."[7]

The pre-Cambrian microbes would have had to do an incredible sprint through evolution not only to develop into nine-foot-long nautiloids but also to develop a human-like eye.

It has to be stated that this section in Steve Jones's book (pp. 271–281) relies heavily on speculation. As previously stated, he poses the question about whether the Cambrian period was a time of great change with no time for selection. And his answer is, "With little doubt, no."

But then come pages of much doubt and uncertainty. They are punctuated with speculative words like "perhaps," "hint at," "hint of," "suggests," and "look rather like." For half the pages, there is a retreat into the chalk fossils and the trenches of World War I. We learn much that is fascinating about the makeup of chalk beds, but nothing to help us understand—with little doubt—how the Cambrian explosion happened suddenly yet left time—millions of years—for slow, gradual evolution.

This is not Steve Jones's strongest argument, the creationists would say.

A STRANGE IRONY

The fossil record is a puzzle. Some stress that the missing links are the weakest link in evolution. We can see why, for some of the above reasons.

And yet some champions of evolutionary like T. H. Huxley and T. H. Morgan still maintain the validity of the fossil record. In his *Critique of the Theory of Evolution*, T. H. Morgan states that the evidence from the earth's strata is "by all the odds the strongest evidence of the theory of evolution."[8] Huxley, Darwin's nineteenth-century counterpart, wrote that "the primary and direct evidence in favor of evolution can be furnished only by paleontology."[9]

But, again, what do you think?

And now to our own family fossil album. How do we all relate to Neanderthal man and Cro-Magnon man, not to mention African Eve and Java man? At times, there seem to be enough human skulls and bones to fill a cemetery. They must help us. Surely!

NOTES:

1. Charles Darwin, "On the imperfection of the geological record," Chapter 10 in *On the Origin of Species* (J. M. Dent & Sons Ltd, 1971), 292–93.

2. Dr. David M. Raup, *Field Museum Bulletin*, vol. 50(1) (January 1979): 22.

3. Steve Jones, *Almost Like a Whale—The Origin of the Species Updated* (Anchor, 2000), 252.

4. Ibid., 254.

5. BBC Horizon program on dinosaurs, April, 2002.

6. Richard Dawkins, as quoted by Philip E. Johnson in *Darwin on Trial* (Monarch Publications, 1991), 54.

7. Bliss, *Fossils: Key to the Present* (Parker and Gish), 29. Quoted in Ian Campbell, *A Case for Creation*, 2000, 23.

8. T. H. Morgan, *A Critique of the Theory of Evolution* (Princeton University Press, 1916).

9. T. H. Huxley, as quoted by Professor H. Enoch, *Evolution or Creation* (Evangelical Press, 1966), 13.

Chapter 11

Our Relatives?

The origins of our family are pretty straightforward. They begin in a warm, wet clearing somewhere in Africa. The first primates swung down from the trees 65 million years ago, when the dinosaurs were evicted by a meteorite megabomb.

Life in those days was lived at a leisurely pace, and the family took its time. Quite a lot, actually. Fifty million years and seven or eight thousand primate species later, the first apes strolled onto life's stage. It took another ten million years before they branched out and expanded the family business into chimps, gorillas, and humans.

Our great, great (etc.) Uncle and Aunt Australopithecus arrived out of Africa around four million years ago. We would have immediately recognized the family resemblance from the neck down, though Aunty could have done with a body wax. Still, Uncle liked her, and that was enough to eventually produce Homo habilis (first tool ancestor?). Not much later, Homo erectus stood proud in the pampas.

This, then, is the family album on view in any of our classrooms and in frequent "home movies" on television. It shows the ape features softening into the more modern look. Thicker-skulled Homo sapiens—that's a technical description, by the way, not an insult—arrived about 150,000 years ago, and the ice age and evolution's fine-tuning department finally produced the shape and cuteness fit for local baby competitions and beauty pageants.

Here, with occasional adjustments, are our roots. This is the simple story we pass on as we sit in our clearings (family rooms), still picking and combing nits and fleas from our offspring while they're distracted by "The Flintstones."

Such is life. Or is it? Alas, life's never really that simple. Hardly a month goes by without one of those "Well, actually ..." scientists raising the latest contradiction or theory. One such is Professor Steve Jones. He now tells us that the family album may, after all, be only wishful thinking. In his rewrite of *On the Origin of Species,* he adds qualifications and even complications.

> As more bones turn up, the story becomes less clear. ... In spite of a century's claims of the discovery of "missing links," it is quite possible that no bone yet found is on the direct genetic line to ourselves. With so many kinds to choose from, so few remains of each, and such havoc among their relics,

none of the fossils may have direct descendants today.[1]

Two hundred years ago, we had it all figured out. There was a garden in Eden, a man and a woman, a rather enjoyable commandment from on high and, hey presto, the human race! That, of course, was given the thumbs down and replaced by the out-of-Africa story above. Now, it seems, not even this is right.

"Not right" is somewhat of an understatement. Truth be known, it's a family-at-war saga, as gripping, underhanded, and dramatic as any military thriller. If only the school textbooks told it as it was, they'd become bestsellers, and pupil boredom would be a thing of the past.

FAMILY AT WAR

The main protagonist is, of course, the majority group who believe the family's ancestors swung out of the trees a few million years ago. The underdogs are those who go for more recent beginnings on the ground, with tree swinging as a fun option. But this is to put it crudely. This battling-good yarn has a rainbow of colorful opponents. This is how *Sunday Telegraph* journalist Julian Coman put it:

> The race to find the evolutionary "missing link" between apes, chimpanzees and humans has never been one for the intellectually squeamish. Few fields of academic endeavor have proved as cut-throat. All kinds

of deceits and tricks have been tried—and more than once.[2]

Here are just some of the combatants and four of the contests.

1. LUCY VERSUS THE REST

The bones of contention in our first ancestor feud are between anthropologists from France and Kenya. The Paris brigade amasses in support of their supposed six-million-year-old creature christened Millennium Ancestor. Ranged against them is an African army of anthropologists fighting for the reputation of three-foot-tall Lucy, a mere slip of a fossil at 3.5 million years old. While Millennium Ancestor was fashioned from a questionable femur, there was a full two-fifths of Lucy on which to gaze. Also threatened by the ancient femur (or was it a hip bone, as some argued?) were Lucy's younger relatives—Nutcracker man (found in 1959) and Handy man (1963).

Incidentally, Lucy was said to walk upright on the basis of a knee joint. However, this was found one mile away

> Lucy was said to walk upright on the basis of a knee joint. However, this was found one mile away from the main skeleton and 200 feet lower in the strata.

from the main skeleton and 200 feet lower in the strata, according to Geoffrey Chapman's "Apes and Men" fact sheet from the Creation Science Movement. Creationist Malcolm Bowden, in his book *Ape Men—Fact or Fallacy?*, claims that Lucy was an ape and quotes support from two distinguished professors.[3]

All this, however, was a mere tiff compared to the next two disputes.

2. TRICKS OF THE TRADE

Here begin the confessions of the frauds or tricks of the paleontology trade. Below, they are set out according to notoriety. But first, a caution. A handful of bad scientists do not, of course, condemn all in white coats.

Piltdown man (1912). An almost complete skull was found on Piltdown Farm near Lewes in Sussex, England. The jaw was definitely apelike. The cranium was definitely human. Here, definitely—at least for forty-one years—was the missing link. It turned out that a hoaxer (a kind description, probably) had used potassium dichromate to age the jaw of an orangutan before filing down the teeth to make them look more human.

Peking (or Pekin) man (1926). Peking was based on twenty-four broken and jawless skulls with cranial capacities judged to be halfway between man and ape. No limb bones were found, so fossil experts decided that Peking man was probably a head-hunting cannibal and these were the remains of two dozen unfortunate victims. The fragmented remains, found near

Peking in China, were eventually reclassified as the leftovers from a human feast on ape brains, after advanced tools and human remains were found at the same site.

Java man (1891). Java was proclaimed to be an upright walking ape, judging from just a skullcap and thighbone. This, together with the above cases, persuaded a whole generation that humans had indeed descended from apes. According to Malcolm Bowden, the man who found Java man confessed before his death that the skull was that of a large gibbon and that the human leg bone was found forty-five feet away. The rather dishonest finder had also hidden the fact that he had excavated modern human remains at the same time in the same place and at the same level. This only came to light after an expedition could find no further trace of Java man.[4]

Stooping Rhodesian man (1921). As we know, the chimp stoops to walk. The reason is that the hip joints are at the back of a pelvic girdle that juts out rearwards. Humans walk upright because their center of gravity goes directly through the pelvic girdle, with the hips in the central position. Rhodesian man's pelvis was incomplete and broken in fragments before it was patched together by an ornithologist. According to Bill Cooper of the Creation Science Movement, the hip joint was given "an entirely false orientation," giving the reconstruction "a rather ridiculous posture, that of having the knees bowed outwards, while the feet (whose originals had not survived) were turned inward."[5] Professor Le Gros Clark is quoted as declaring, "The result of the disorientation is not only grotesque but to the eye of the mammalian anatomist, impossible."[6]

Today, Rhodesian man enjoys full membership among Homo sapiens.

Neanderthal man. Many will know Mr. Neanderthal well after spending several nights in his company, courtesy of a television reconstruction in 2001.[7] We ate, slept, and played with him and his family, and we were assured it was authentic by the presence of adviser Professor Chris Stringer, lead paleontologist at the Natural History Museum. But the presentation of Neanderthal man as our ancestor angers creationists. They insist that Homo sapiens' remains have been found at lower strata than Neanderthal. They believe that he was no more than a "degenerate variety of Homo sapiens with a larger brain, and suffering from rickets, osteoarthritis, and syphilis."[8]

The creationists have an abiding anger about television soaps based on a few old bones and tools. They liken it to the fantasy of BBC's television series *Walking with Dinosaurs,* similarly reconstructed from bones and Disney-like fantasy digitals.

We were treated to views of Neanderthal groups lying together picking fleas from one another's hair, while the commentary explained that Neanderthals spent as much as four hours a day in this pleasurable pursuit. Viewers were also promised scenes of mating by the dominant male, while lower-ranking folk try to join the party. Could there be any archaeological basis for such behavior? No, but we do know that present-day apes indulge in those sorts of things. Evolution dogma requires that Neanderthals be primitive, too.[9]

Nebraska man. He began as a tooth and ended up as a family man in *London Illustrated News.* Unfortunately, some years later, further excavations revealed that the tooth was that of a pig. According to evolutionists, this reconstruction was unfortunate, but nevertheless they approve the process of building up pictures from bits and pieces as an educated and useful skill.

Not so the creationists. They believe the art of reconstruction is a scandal. Malcolm Bowden explains, "In each case ... the drawings by various artists based on the same skull are completely different, proving that these pictures are figments of the imagination." Bowden reproduces the examples in his books.[10]

3. YOU SAY "MILLIONS" AND HE SAYS "A THOUSAND"

This particular battle zone involves allegations of a cover-up and is based on what was found in the bowels of the London Natural History Museum. Creationists make two specific charges in one of their pamphlets.[11]

First, a "vast body of evidence" contrary to evolution lies undisclosed in places like the Natural History Museum. If conventional geological time spans are accepted, this evidence from the fossil record "shows that man has been around millions of years." In this case, something somewhere is very wrong. This accusation is aimed at faulty dating as much as the fossil evidence and comes from leading Creation Science Movement writer Bill Cooper.

However, when I spoke to the museum's paleontology leader, Professor Stringer, about this, he said that this was not true. Mr. Cooper had made a mistake, especially in the second charge he had made.

This involves Miocene man, a human skeleton that lies encased in Miocene limestone, dated at up to 24 million years before the supposed emergence of humans, claims Bill Cooper. He adds, "This skeleton was dug out of the Lower Miocene deposits of Grande Terre, part of the Caribbean Island of Guadeloupe." Mr. Cooper adds that it has been in the possession of the museum for 170 years, and "during the early nineteenth century it was displayed as a curiosity. ... However, once Darwinism gained a foothold in academic circles, it seems that the specimen was quietly removed from public display."

Professor Stringer told me, "Bill Cooper is right when he says that the specimen was from Guadeloupe, which is largely Miocene. However, what he hasn't taken account of is that Guadeloupe is fringed with Quaternary rock [modern deposits] from where the specimen has been taken. The body is probably no more than one thousand years old."

Enter John Layton, who mans the Creation Science Movement's Genesis Expo Centre in Portsmouth. He states that the museum is wrong. "We still stand by Bill Cooper's pamphlet, as does he. We still distribute it. If it were wrong we would have removed it from our list."

Malcolm Bowden e-mailed me: "It is clear that evolutionists have thrown up a great deal of mud to cover over this difficult fossil. The encasing material is harder than marble and I cannot believe it could be a recently formed beach rock; that is hardly likely to be as hard as this."

This battle zone flared up again when creationist geologist David Tyler was critical of Miocene man. He had analyzed the rock around the skeleton and found it to be beach rock.[12] Professor Stringer was delighted to recommend his paper. However, David Tyler is the only creationist to take this line, as far as I can discover, and Malcolm Bowden and Bill Cooper declare that Mr. Tyler is wrong in his work. They quote another geologist, John Mackay, who has been out to the island, "and found that the strata the skeleton was in ran under the nearby hills and was not therefore a recent beach rock."

No doubt this battle will rage on until somebody finds a foolproof way of taking a rock sample back to Guadeloupe to compare it with what is there. Of course, this can't be done because they cannot agree on dating methods. As far as creationists are concerned, both rocks and man are only thousands of years old, and Miocene man shows the fallacy surrounding the dating game.

> Turkmenian plateau contains more than 3,000 footprints ... but the most mysterious fact is that among the footprints of dinosaurs, footprints of bare human feet were found.

4. MAN WALKING WITH DINOSAURS?

Man's ancestors and dinosaurs could not possibly have co-existed. The fossil evidence and the geological ages do not permit it. Primates originated, as stated previously, no earlier than 65 million years ago, when a meteorite cleared the way for them by wiping out the dinosaurs. This has always been the standard reply to creationist claims that human-like footprints have been found in those of dinosaurs.

At least it was until April 2002, when *Nature* revealed that man's ancestors came down from the trees and walked with dinosaurs for 20 million years. This shocking news, of course, is still highly controversial, but *Nature* at least gave critical acceptance to the study by an Anglo-Swiss-American team.[13] It is "based on a statistical analysis of the fossil evidence," reports Roger Highfield in *The Daily Telegraph,* who adds that "the study supports previously disputed findings from several evolutionary trees for mammals, using molecular evidence."[14]

All this sounds quite respectable until one realizes that these battle zones are all fought on the flimsiest of evidence.

Dr. Martin of the above-mentioned team explained, "Our calculations indicate that we have fossil evidence for only about five percent of extinct primates and so it's as if paleontologists have been trying to reconstruct a 1,000-piece jigsaw puzzle using just fifty pieces."

No doubt this battle is not over. How could it be when such vast theories are based on such venial data?

Likewise, the creationist evidence is flimsy, but at least it is as plausible as the evolutionists'. See what you think.

Turkmenian plateau contains more than 3,000 footprints ... but the most mysterious fact is that among the footprints of dinosaurs, footprints of bare human feet were found.[15] Record of the Rocks, a creationist Web site, states that this sighting must be added to the Taylor Tracks in America, showing "Fourteen human tracks with dino tracks, plus another five sightings of human tracks with alleged prehistoric creatures."[16]

The evidence is flimsy and not well documented, and

therefore questionable. They go on from this to quote experts, one of whom is Ernst Mayr of Harvard, along the following lines:

> Creationists have stated that humans and
> dinosaurs were contemporaries in time. ...
> Were this momentous statement true the
> names of its discoverers would thunder down
> the corridors of time as individuals who made
> one of the most outstanding discoveries of the
> twentieth century.[17]

NOTES:

1. Steve Jones, *Almost Like a Whale* (Anchor, 2000), 427.

2. Julian Coman, *The Sunday Telegraph,* February 4, 2001.

3. Malcolm Bowden, *Ape Men: Fact or Fallacy?* (3rd reprint), chapter 8.

4. Ibid., chapter 6.

5. William Cooper, "The Stooping Rhodesian Man Fraud," Pamphlet 307 (Creation Science Movement, July 1996), 3.

6. Ibid.

7. ITV Channel 4, December 2001.

8. www.creationsciencemovement.com.journal-Jan-2001.htm.

9. Ibid.

10. Malcolm Bowden, *Ape Men: Fact or Fallacy?*, chapter 1.

11. William Cooper, "Miocene Man," Pamphlet 234 (Creation Science Movement, revised, January 1986).

12. The BCS Symposium "Understanding Fossils and Earth's History," D. Tyler ed., 1984 special issue,.

13. The team was made up of Dr. Robert Martin, of the Field Museum, Chicago; Dr. Simon Tavare, of the University of Southern California; and Dr. Christopher Soligo, of London's Natural History Museum.

14. Roger Highfield, *Daily Telegraph,* April 18, 2002. See also *Nature,* April 2002.

15. Reported in *Komsomolskaya Pravda,* Russia, 1995.

16. www.bible.ca/tracksdp-geol-column.htm.

17. Ernst Mayr in the Gish—Mayr debate, Evansville, Indiana.

Chapter 12

Small Wonders
of Our World

My pet worm is amazing. Halipegus—that's its Sunday name—has fascinated me for a decade, and even co-starred with a serial killer in a creation/evolution novel of mine.[1] Its fascinating life cycle begins under the tongue of the green frog. It then climbs to the roof of the mouth and hangs about before eventually ejecting, as a hermaphrodite, its own fertilized eggs, which are then digested by the host. Excreted into the water, they hatch into microscopic water babes with tiny beaks strong enough to break and enter the shell of a fingernail-sized ramshorn snail.

Once inside the ramshorn snail, our worm enjoys a feast of its new host's liver and eventually departs the ex-snail to hunt out its next meal ticket. As our microscopic Rambo comes to rest on the pond floor, it sprouts tentacles from its tail to lure a water flea called cyclops.

Amazingly, Halipegus coils like a spring in its own tail and patiently awaits a nibble. A passing cyclops flea merely has to open its mouth in curiosity and our worm launches itself down the gullet, through the intestinal walls to the safety of a body cavity. Not the stomach, mind you, because Rambo is now rather vulnerable to gastric acids. Our worm's aim and catapult strength has to be precise. No time for trial and experiment. Too weak, and the flea will have fled. Too strong, and Halipegus will be back fishing, surrounded by an increasing pile of deceased fleas with see-through bodies.

Once inside a safe cavity in its new mobile home, our worm hardly has time to decorate before it and the host become a fine meal for a dragonfly larva. This, in turn, gets eaten by the green frog, and Halipegus, understandably, begins to feel at home, especially because it has now developed a "diving suit" to protect it from green frog gastric juices. All it now has to do is to climb a Mount Everest, back up the gut, to start the life cycle all over again under the host's tongue. Four lives flitting to four separate homes, and every Halipegus is programmed to repeat this life cycle.

"It stretches the imagination to such an extent that you can't believe it could possibly have evolved," says worm expert Professor Miriam Rothschild. "There must be a humorous designer somewhere who has arranged the whole thing for his own amusement."[2]

Is she right? Was it designed? Could not Halipegus and its life cycle have happened by chance? Maybe there's a third alternative. Once the Big Bang happened, an inescapable recipe or formula was set in motion that meant that earth and life and Halipegus just could not be avoided.

An intelligent designer? Blind chance? An unavoidable necessity? Who or what is responsible for the incredible complexity that surrounds us in life? Even leading Darwinist and atheist Richard Dawkins concedes, "Biology is the study of complicated things that give the appearance of having been designed for a purpose."[3]

Of course, Professor Dawkins is only teasing. The subtitle of the book with that quote reads, "Why the evidence of evolution reveals a universe without design." We will tackle this fascinating contest of ideas in chapter 13. For now, let's recapture the wonder of our amazing world. Let's see what the argument is all about.

INSTINCT

Halipegus homes in on four hosts. But, of course, other creatures can match if not surpass this. The salmon swims the globe in search of the pink shrimp from which it gets its distinctive color. On sexual maturity, it heads back to spawn in its own birth pool in the quiet upper reaches of some remote river. It does so with the amazing ability to switch from sea to fresh water, leaping in the face of incredible currents.

Most of the 80,000 moths and butterflies migrate thousands of miles. Two experts writing for a Creation Science pamphlet explain:

The monarch butterfly of America dies after it

has laid its eggs in the Southern States, but the generation of butterflies that emerge from the pupal state return to those parts of North America whence the parents came. There are certain trees on the route that these butterflies have followed for countless generations, on which they have rested on their journey."[4]

Steve Jones tells of groups of organisms whose behavior adds up to more than what each individual is programmed to do in its DNA. For example, a colony of brainless sea anemones can declare civil war on a neighboring cluster of individual anemones who, in turn, each enlist in their own well-drilled army of counterterrorism. Ants and termites and all other creatures are programmed in the genes to abide by one set of instincts or another, yet the group instinct

> Highly complex machines power our bodies. It is impossible to see how they ever evolved. To work, they need all the parts present and working at full capacity. Take one cog away, or alter it in any other way, and the machine would grind to a useless halt.

seems to be above and beyond the selfish needs of its own personal genes.

Both creationists and evolutionists highlight the beehive as perhaps the epitome of group instinct. At the heart of the hive is the biggest mystery of all collectives: that 15,000 bees in an average hive should give up the one thing that normally drives all living creatures—sex! This is sacrificed by the vast majority, and only a few drones engage in hanky-panky with a single queen, who can live up to thirty years. Every bee has its own task, and that can change according to its age. There are midwives and undertakers. Bouncers deal with those who've had one over the eight nectar dips, and a cross between the Special Air Service and the Royal Air Force daily mount a Battle-of-Britain-type defense of the hive. The youngest have to earn their wings with mop and bucket, but once qualified they can graduate from cleaning to foraging missions.

These are the hunters who dive-bomb to targets given them in the communications room. Television's nature programs often show us the coded wiggles and waltzes of a bee scout who has previously located a food target. A circle dance means food is near. A figure-eight reel means a long-distance mission. Encoded in the wild wiggles are navigational directions to the target flowers in relation to the sun and the hive, plus distance to be traveled. All this was discovered by Karl von Frisch in 1946, but not even he knew how bees followed the wild dancing. It couldn't be eyesight because every bee around would make a beeline to smother the poor target. Furthermore, the bees were able to get the message even at midnight dances. And when they got the message, only two or three bees followed up the directions.

Thanks to Professor Axel Michelson of Odense University in Denmark, we now know. He studied his dancing bees by placing millimeter-long microphones beside them. He reported to the 2002 British Association annual meeting in May that the bees were emitting waves of air pressure that were even above normal legal limits for industry—at 94 decibels. However, the wave burst traveled only short distances so that no more than two or three bees got the message. Professor Michelson discovered this when he invented his own computerized robot bee. He told the conference, "When we brought it [the robot] into the hive and made it dance, a number of bees obeyed the instructions given by the dancer. For example, they would fly 500 meters to the south if we told them to."

The bees, not having any "hearing" organs, picked up the instructions through their antennae by gauging the airflow changes. In addition to this, the bee has one other aid: On a good day, you or I might just catch the aroma of a rose at arm's length. A bee can detect it across a crowded football field.

Is all of this a sign of design implanted in bee genes from the very start, or could bees have evolved this sophistication by chance? Maybe they had no alternative but to obey a Big Bang formula? And if they evolved their wild dancing, what did they do for food while they were working on their routine? Or have we missed some other unknown explanation?

While on bees, what about pollination and the plants? Of course, we're now moving away from instincts and on to our next wonder: the complexity of systems at the very heart of nature. There are systems that seem to be so complex that if anything were slightly different or any part were removed, they would cease to function. For example, what came first: bees or plants? It seems that neither could exist without the other. So did they coincidentally and simultaneously evolve together, or were they all created together at one time? Design or chance?

IRREDUCIBLE COMPLEXITY

Highly complex machines power our bodies. It is impossible to see how they ever evolved. To work, they need all the parts present and working at full capacity. Take one cog away, or alter it in any other way, and the machine would grind to a useless halt. This was the claim of Professor Michael Behe in his influential book *Darwin's Black Box.* Here, we abbreviate just one of the many examples used by Behe to illustrate what he calls irreducible complexities—the blood clotting mechanism. Behe asks us to consider whether the following could have evolved by chance, step by step, or whether it is evidence for an intelligent designer, who produced it all together.

The human body is a pressurized system. Puncture it and your eight pints of blood could drain away—a very real risk with hemophilia. However, the blood-system defenses are on autopilot, and the clotting mechanism kick-starts itself at the slightest pinprick. Of course, it must only heal across the wound and then immediately stop. If it carried on, unwanted clots could break away to the heart or head, with fatal consequences. Overclotting might also close off a vital blood flow. However, it cannot afford to knock off too soon or the job won't be finished. The clotting mechanism has to be split-second in timing. Anything short of perfection just will not do.

The rest of the mechanism also requires perfection. First,

imagine a microscopic set of barbells—a bar with weights at either end. Then, add another set of weights at the center of the bar. This is fibrinogen—easy to remember because it is this protein that forms the fibers that crisscross the wound. In peace time, it minds its own business and relaxes on a round-the-body cruise. When under wound attack, a "circular saw" protein missile called thrombin roars around, lopping off parts of the "weights" of fibrinogen to expose sticky patches. Fibrinogen now shrinks to become fibrin. This, with its sticky patches, seeks and finds other fibrin to stick to. Together, they form long chains, making a fishnet pattern across the wound to entrap the blood cells.

So far, so good, but what about all those vicious thrombin "circular saws" running rampant? If something doesn't stop them, all the blood in the body will solidify into one massive clot. Well, there's antithrombin to switch it off, and you won't be too surprised to know that there is a whole army of activities needed to get antithrombin to do its simple job. This could take up a chapter on its own, but now we need to go back a bit.

Before the wound attack, thrombin was a switched-off "circular saw" called prothrombin. Another protein called the Stuart factor is used to start up the "circular saw" but, of course, that means the Stuart factor also needs to be controlled. If it weren't, it would activate the prothrombin, which would then slice off the end of fibrinogen, which would then turn into fibrin, which would then clot all the blood in the organism.

So, what controls the Stuart factor in this incredible blood-clotting cascade? It has an accomplice called accelerin. But, hang on, what keeps this dynamic duo apart? Well, accelerin is normally inactive as—yes, you've guessed it—proaccelerin.

Now, here comes the surprise twist. What knocks the "pro" off proaccelerin to make it work? You'll never guess this one. It's our "circular-saw" protein, thrombin!

Now, it might help you to throw the book at a convenient wall at this moment, and that would be perfectly understandable. This is nonsense! How can thrombin, which is at the end of our chain reaction, be there at the very beginning? It's like having my new granddaughter Lois turn up on my wedding night thirty-three years ago to tell me how to produce her father.

Hopefully, you've retrieved this book and we can now continue. It turns out that because of a little sluggishness in the system, there's always a few "circular saws" of thrombin "revving" away in the background, and some even manage to escape being turned off by antithrombin.

At this stage, you have mastered the yellow and green Central &

We could wonder at how feathers could develop from scales, which are made of different material. And if they did evolve through fraying, how did fuzzy, handicapped dinosaurs survive millions of years looking as if they'd been dragged through a hedge backwards?

District lines of our blood-clotting system. I hesitate to take you on the Piccadilly, Northern, and Victoria lines of this incredible under-the-surface blood-clotting system, which would require at least two more pages. For those braver, who would like to know how rat poison, Vitamin K, and amino acids are added, go to page 83 of Behe's book, and our thoughts and encouragement go with you.

For us mere mortals, Professor Behe's point is made. The blood-clotting mechanism is so complex that if you take any one part of it away, it won't work. Also, it appears to be an impossibility to build it up step by step through evolution.

Chance? Necessity? Design?

AND FINALLY ...

We should allow space for the trillions of tiny motors that power our bodies, rotating 100 times every second, each being 200,000 times smaller than a pinhead. "ATP synthase" won a joint 1997 Nobel Prize for America's Paul Boyer and the U.K.'s John Walker, and you will be pleased to know that it has just supplied your brain and eyes with the energy to read this sentence.

We could also spend a whole chapter detailing the three types of feathers and their highly complicated "Velcro" hooks and barbules. The complexity of wings and feathers makes the blood-clotting cascade look like kindergarten stuff. We could wonder at how dinosaur scales began to fray and flop about until they eventually turned into feathers. We could wonder at how feathers could develop from scales, which are made of different material. And if they did evolve through fraying, how did fuzzy, handicapped dinosaurs survive millions of years looking as if they'd been dragged through a hedge backwards?

But perhaps we should use the remaining space for a creationist's favorite—the flame-throwing bombardier beetle, highlighted in 1987 (Pamphlet 233) by the chairman of the Creation Science Movement, Dr. David Rosevear. It also featured in the Proceedings of the National Academy of Sciences in 2002 as a research paper by Professor Thomas Eisner and Dr. Daniel Aneshansley of Cornell University.

Briefly, bombardier (Brachinus) machine guns emit boiling chemicals out of rear gun turrets at 212°F, at up to 1,000 pulses per second. Roger Highfield in *The Daily Telegraph* likened it to a "pulsed rocket mechanism very similar to that of a V-1 or doodle-bug, the first operational cruise missile the Germans used to bomb England in the Second World War."

Eisner and Aneshansley used flash photography to capture the incredible accuracy and reaction of bombardier as they put it through target practice. There is hardly any point on its body that cannot be touched without causing a rapid burst, and this creates the first vexing mystery. Every time the beetle attacks, it cannot help but drench itself with hot corrosive elements that would burn our skins white in seconds. How does it survive?

Within its centimeter-long body, our beetle has chambers to store substitute hydroquinones, tolylhydroquinone, and hydrogen peroxide. These chemicals mix peacefully unless high temperatures are reached. The chambers feed into a mixing reservoir that again lets into a combustion chamber that sports two gun turrets. At the slightest sign of danger, a charge of chemicals is squirted into the chamber where incredibly complex enzyme molecules encourage the chemicals to bond explosively out of the turrets. Now, the creationist asks a series of questions:

❖ How could bombardier have evolved by chance?

❖ Why should a beetle start to develop storage chambers in its body?

❖ Why then fill them with highly corrosive chemicals?

❖ How did it fashion highly complex enzymes that bind the chemicals into a bomb?

❖ On discovering how to explode the mixture, how did it survive long enough to pass the knowledge on to its offspring?

❖ When did bombardier hit on a combustion chamber plus gun turrets?

❖ Having gotten it all together, what about the internal communications system?

This last point is crucial. Defense systems are good, but an amorous Mrs. Bombardier would not have appreciated a sudden loss of control by her mate. Passion is one thing. White-hot heat exploding from the nether regions is quite another.

Chance? Design? The result of an unstoppable, automatic recipe or formula? This is the big debate of our time, and our next chapter. It's quite fascinating.

NOTES:

1. Kevin Logan, *Survival of the Fittest* (HarperCollins, 1999). Distributed now through www.thisischristchurch. org.uk.

2. Professor Miriam Rothschild, who featured Halipegus as her contribution to *Wonders of Science,* ITV, March 1994.

3. Richard Dawkins, *The Blind Watchmaker* (Penguin Books, 1987).

4. E. Johannsen and T. W. Carron, "Instincts and Creation," Pamphlet 291 (Creation Science Movement, 1993).

Chapter 13

Revolution

Chapter 13, and we're looking at chance. Spooky or what? Or is it chance? Perhaps I designed the book this way? Or maybe there is a previously unknown literary rule that authors who tackle creation and evolution for Cook Communications will necessarily always use chapter 13 to focus on chance.

CHANCE, DESIGN, OR NECESSITY. WHICH?

To be honest, detailed planning is not my strong point. You, me, Halipegus, the bombardier beetle, and even this planet—are we all designed, are we accidental chance happenings, or are we the necessary outworking of this universe as it is?

A friend is involved in sorting out the latest railway crash as

🔍

> ❖ There is a slow but recognizable revolution at the heart of our culture. At its axis is this big issue of origins. It is a wheel with three spokes—chance, design, and necessity.

we go to press. He has three choices as to cause:

❖ Design: Did somebody deliberately sabotage the points that caused the crash? Were some of the bolts unscrewed by a vandal with technical know-how and tools?

❖ Chance: Was the crash just one of those freak accidents that nobody could have foreseen? Nobody's fault. Nobody meant it to happen. Just one of those things.

❖ Necessity: Did it happen because of the rail system itself? And this is crucial for my friend because this is his brief. Is the rail system so organized in Britain that this crash was an accident waiting to happen?

Here is the heart of our book, and the main reason for writing it. There is a slow but recognizable revolution at the heart of our culture. At its axis is this big issue of origins. It is a wheel with three spokes—chance, design, and necessity. It is not a new phenomenon. This revolution is always turning, and what hits the road in one culture will be different from what happens in another. It depends on two things: the age in which you live and your geography.

ACROSS THE AGES

The ancient Greeks wrestled with this issue. Epicurus, celebrated chance and, like Darwin, believed that forces of nature caused different types of organisms to arise, allowing only the best to survive. Epicurus might have been the star of our book had he beat Darwin to the idea that evolution happened through natural selection.

Opposition came from the Stoics, who celebrated a mixture of design and necessity. The gods, they believed, had left nothing to chance. There was a divine order to the universe, and they must live according to it.

Take now a massive leap in time to Francis Bacon, who cut

Previously, the queen of the sciences had been theology. Soon, theology was to be pauper. An enlightened England drifted from a culture based on a designing God to a world that emphasized necessity because it had to follow natural laws.

the apron strings attached to sixteenth-century England, saying it was now old enough to go and find its own way. In the process, he unwittingly began to move a design-based society toward chance and necessity.

He taught that knowledge should be gained through testing and tasting and experience, not because Mother Church said so. Previously, the queen of the sciences had been theology. Soon, theology was to be pauper. An enlightened England drifted from a culture based on a designing God to a world that emphasized necessity because it had to follow natural laws. One man, René ("I think therefore I am") Descartes believed that all was necessary (and also designed) because the whole universe was a mechanism wound up by a divine being, who then left it to its own ends (deism).

> Culture had generally come to accept the partial truth that knowledge could only come through the laboratory or logic. Most theologians bowed to this and increasingly worked under it in order to retain credibility.

Isaac Newton's genius for discovering the laws that necessarily governed life was turned by his disciples into the relentless, mechanistic world of the Industrial Revolution. By 1854, Charles Dickens could have his *Hard Times* headmaster,

Gradgrind, treating his pupils as mere cogs or miniature robots. Already the wheel had begun to turn toward chance, and Charles Darwin published *On the Origin of Species* just five years later.

Culture had generally come to accept the partial truth that knowledge could only come through the laboratory or logic. Most theologians bowed to this and increasingly worked under it in order to retain credibility. Mainstream theology was, for instance, quick to accept both Hutton's necessary geological ages and Darwin's theory of chance evolution. However, in the last two decades, our culture has begun to revolve back towards design. But more of this later.

This revolution turns not only with time but also with different geography.

ACROSS THE GLOBE

Necessity often reigns in developing nations. Kismet and fate program Middle East spiritualities onto the railway tracks of destiny. Reincarnation ties Far East believers to the endless Wheel of Samsara (also rolling West with increasing influence). Villagers around Bethany, an orphanage in Tanzania I help to oversee, are governed by spirits and witch doctors. These are, to those involved, necessary to the very fabric of existence. This is the way life is.

In the West, chance reigns. It used to be the pure roulette wheel of evolution both for the earth and for life. Now, fashion rolls on because things increasingly look designed, especially the universe itself. Its settings appear finely calibrated so as to produce and sustain life on earth. Consequently, many who want to cling to chance have come up with another idea—multiple universes. There must have been billions of universes, they claim. We just happen to have hit the jackpot, and ours is fine-tuned to produce life. This is now the most popular noncreator explanation of origins in today's culture, if our earlier pub survey is any guide.

> Despite the modern love affair with chance and necessity, design is growing in popularity in the West.

Once you have your necessary fine-tuned universe, it will tend to include something like one of the following:

❖ Daniel Dennett's uncreated, mindless, mechanical recipe for life (an algorithm) that, once set in motion, cannot stop or do anything else, except what it is programmed to do.[1]

❖ Richard Dawkins's Selfish Gene that exists only to reproduce itself, and uses everything else, such as the human body, as a vehicle of convenience.[2]

❖ Stephen Wolfram's computer-program idea. A British physicist, he states in his 2002 book *A New Kind of Science* that nature uses simple computer programs to build up complex patterns and shapes. All 848 pages of his book are full of them. He believes his way will overtake Darwin's natural selection, adding poignantly, "I've come to have some sympathy with creationists. Natural selection isn't everything, after all.[3]

A universe of pure chance was championed by existential-ist philosophers and writers like Jean-Paul Sartre. He once famously proclaimed that "we were mere accidental bubbles floating aimlessly through space." Nobel prize winner Jacques Monod, a French biochemist, saw nothing but chance in the light of evolution, writing, "Man at last knows he is alone in the unfeeling immensity of the universe, out of which he has emerged by chance."[4]

Despite the modern love affair with chance and necessity, design is growing in popularity in the West. So, too, is a rather cleverly designed hybrid of chance and necessity. It is as though the wheel of culture has been unraveled so that everything hits the road at once. It is to this first that we briefly turn.

NECESSARY CHANCE BY DESIGN

I'd better start by unpacking this subheading. This is the idea that God necessarily had to design His universe with chance built into its very fabric. Former Cambridge Professor of Mathematical Physics John Polkinghorne, now an Anglican clergyman, proposes that God uses the element of chance in an ongoing creative process. He didn't just "light the blue touch paper for the Big Bang," but He is "as much Creator today as he was fifteen billion years ago."[5] But God has a dilemma. He is faithful and therefore wants to provide reliability in His uni-verse. He's also a God of love who, like a good parent, wants to grant freedom and independence to His children. He gives the "twin gifts of independence and reliability" in His creation, which "provides a fruitful interplay of chance and necessity in evolving cosmic history."[6] This prevents Him from being a God of the extremes—the puppet master pulling the strings, or the indifferent spectator.

This contrasts with the creationist, who believes God created all in a working week, and knows exactly what the past, present, and future is. This is the God who foremost is the designer. Chance is not an option.

Polkinghorne adds, "An evolutionary world is to be understood theologically as a world allowed by the Creator to make itself to a large degree. ... Chance is the sign of freedom, not blind purpose-lessness."[7] He quotes another clergyman, Arthur Peacocke, who states that chance is "the search radar of God, sweeping through all the possible targets of its probing."[8]

Evidence of chance in God's creation can be seen, Polkinghorne believes, in quantum physics. "Once two electrons have interacted with each other they possess a power to influence each other, however widely they subse-quently separate."[9] Chaos Theory is another example. Chance is famously illustrated by the stirrings of an African butterfly's wings causing weather consequences several weeks later in London. Consequently, while God had humanity in mind when He designed His universe, the fact that we've ended up with, say, five digits on each hand is the result of chance.

In the midst of chance, God can allow His people and Himself to act. With chance, God allows Himself to break through the mechanics of His universe to answer prayer or to raise His Son from the dead. All that God cannot do is know the future because "the future is not yet there to be known."[10]

This, writes Polkinghorne, even allows us a new look at the age-old problem of how suffering and evil originated. They are necessary outworkings of the design. He explains: "I do not believe that God directly wills either the act of a murderer, or the incidence of a cancer. I believe he allows both to happen in a creation to which he has given the gift of being itself."[11]

This contrasts with the creationist, who believes God created all in a working week, and knows exactly what the past, present, and future is. This is the God who foremost is the designer. Chance is not an option. The eye, the wing, the bombardier beetle, the universe, and so on, are all preplanned and preordained. This is not a God who has to wait for stars to produce the necessary heavy atoms needed for His universe. This is one who says, "Let there be light," and there is light. He speaks, and that's that. This is a God who has given freedom and reliability, but He Himself is free to adjust the earth laws He has made if He wishes to do so. God is not limited in any of His actions. Evil and suffering are the results of angels and then humans choosing to willfully wreck God's perfect design by wanting to be gods themselves.

However, both parties are of one mind as far as design is concerned. Whether it be Polkinghorne's qualified version, or the full-blooded creationist variety, they want a much greater emphasis on design. And now they are joined by the new breed of radical scientists.

FULL CIRCLE?

The last time culture rested mainly on design was in the Dark Ages. Now it's enjoying a large-scale revival, and those leading it insist we're entering a new age of light and understanding. Tipping the revolution in favor of design are the intellectual arguments of the radical scientists. The creationists are delighted to sit in their slipstream.

> If any one of the dozens of physical laws were fractionally different, this universe would not exist.

Noncreationist Professor Michael Behe is in the forefront of a growing movement that has been so impressive as to earn its own capital initials— Intelligent Design. In 1999, he was joined by Associate Professor Stephen C. Meyer and Dr. William A. Dembski to present papers on "Science and Evidence for Design in the Universe" for the prestigious Proceedings of the Wethersfield Institute in New York.

They, and countless others, are not only arguing for small examples of complexity, like the blood-clotting cascade; they want recognition on a universal scale. They agree that the universe is fine-tuned, but offer what they believe to be a far better explanation than others.

Stephen Meyer leads the charge by tackling those who have already used this fine-tuning argument to propose multiple universes:

> First, all current cosmological models
> involving multiple universes require some
> kind of mechanism for generating universes.
> Yet such a "universe generator" would itself
> require precisely configured physical states,
> thus begging the question of its original
> design. ... Second ... we should prefer
> hypotheses "that are natural extrapolations
> from what we already know" about causal
> powers ... multiple-worlds hypothesis fails
> this test, whereas the theistic-design hypoth-
> esis does not.[12]

Meyer is actually quoting R. Collins within the above quotation. He goes on to say how the point is illustrated. Collins asks his reader to imagine a paleontologist who assumes the existence of an electromagnetic "dinosaur-bone-producing field," as opposed to actual dinosaurs, as an explanation for the origin of large fossilized bones.[13]

The fine-tuning theory is known as the Anthropic Principle—everything fine-tuned to provide life to humankind (from the Greek word *anthropoi*). If any one of the dozens of physical laws were fractionally different, this universe would not exist. These laws include:

- ❖ Expansion of the universe. The slightest fraction faster and it would not have been able to form stars. A tiny fraction slower and it would have rapidly collapsed back in on itself.[14]

- ❖ The gravitational constant has to be 6.67×10^{-11}.

- ❖ The electron charge-to-mass ratio is 1.76×10^{11}.

- ❖ Planck's constant has to be at 6.63×10^{-34} Joules-seconds.

Michael Denton, in *Nature's Destiny* (1998), gives many more examples, pointing out that each has to be fine-tuned. The possibility of getting even one constant right by chance, the so-called "original phase-space volume," is one part in ten billion multiplied to the power of 123. This was the calculation of Oxford physicist Roger Penrose.[15]

Suppose God were to lend you His Universe-Creating Machine, suggests John Polkinghorne in *Quarks, Chaos and Christianity*. You fine-tune your designer universe with your own personal selection of forces and fancies. He adds:

> Right! All the knobs are set, you pull the handle and out comes the universe God has allowed you to create. You wait to see what happens. You'll have to be patient, it may take billions of years. ... We now understand that unless you had set these knobs very precisely

... the world you had decided to create would
have had a very dull and sterile history. It
would not have produced anything like such
interesting consequences as you and me. We
live in a very special universe—one in a trillion
you might say.[16]

So strong is this argument that many believe there is no
competition. There should be no other runners. Commentator
Clifford Longley put it like this:

What it points to is of such an order of certainty
that in any other sphere of science, it would be
regarded as settled. To insist otherwise is like
insisting that Shakespeare was not written by
Shakespeare because it might have been written
by a billion monkeys sitting at a billion key-
boards typing for a billion years. So it might.
But the sight of scientific atheists clutching at
such desperate straws has put new spring in the
step of theists.[17]

At present, Intelligent Design is gaining ground over all
other explanations for our origins. But, of course, this is not the
end of the story. And, of course, we remember that there is no
way of proving beyond doubt that an intelligent designer really
does exist. Atheists still prefer their own explanations, and
some of them even agree that they also know there is no way of
proving beyond doubt that they are right.

However, what the Intelligent Design followers believe was
supported by one of their venerable forerunners nearly 2,000

years ago: "For since the creation of the world God's invisible qualities—his eternal power and divine nature—have been clearly seen, being understood from what has been made, so that men are without excuse."[18]

This, from the apostle Paul's letter to the Romans, leads us into the specifically Christian approach to creation and evolution. Again, we find differences of opinion. Sometimes the disputes are hotter than they should be.

NOTES:

1. Daniel Dennett, *Darwin's Dangerous Idea* (The Penguin Press, 1995).

2. Richard Dawkins, *The Selfish Gene* (Oxford University Press, 1976).

3. Stephen Wolfram, *A New Kind of Science,* Wolfram Media (Telegraph Direct Books on 0870 155 7222). The quotation was taken from *The Daily Telegraph,* May 15, 2002.

4. John Polkinghorne, *Quarks, Chaos and Christianity* (Triangle, 1994), 40. Quoted by Jacques Monod, *Chance and Necessity* (Collins, 1972).

5. John Polkinghorne, *Quarks, Chaos and Christianity,* 37.

6. Ibid., 42.

7. Ibid., 43.

8. Ibid., 42.

9. Ibid., 55.

10. Ibid., 73.

11. Ibid., 47.

12. Stephen Meyer, "Evidence for Design in Physics and Biology," from The Proceedings of the Wethersfield Institute, 1999, 63.

13. Ibid. Also, R. Collins, "The Fine-Tuning Design Argument: A Scientific Argument for the Existence of

God," in M. Murray (ed.), *Reason for Hope Within*, (Eerdmans, 1999), 61.

14. Stephen Meyer explains that the expansion rate of the universe must be calculated to one part in 1060.14. If it had changed by one part either way, it would not have worked. See note 5, p. 60.

15. Quoted by Stephen Meyer. As note 12, p. 61.

16. As note 5, p. 27.

17. As note 12, p. 65.

18. Romans 1:20.

❖ EVIDENCE
FROM SCRIPTURE

Chapter 14

And So to Genesis

S ome would insist that Scripture should have been our start-
ing point right from the beginning. Go first to the "Book of
God's Words" (as John Calvin and Francis Bacon called the
Bible) before opening the "Book of God's Works" (their
description of nature). But, of course, as soon as we do open the
Bible, we hit the problem—Genesis 1!

Most inquiring Christians have increasingly scoured the
many works of God trying to make sense of His mysterious first
words. In this, they believe science has been their friend and
interpreter. Other Christians have done it in reverse: Scripture
first, expecting science to conform or be the foe. A third group
has tried to balance the books and reach a concord between science and religion.

Generally speaking, each camp has long ago dug in and

become entrenched. They no longer communicate, except to exchange rounds of fire in the daily or religious newspapers. Sometimes, they come wrapped "in Christian love." Occasionally, they are barbed with sarcasm—or worse, "devil's work" accusations.

And now for confession time. We humans like to think this subject is wholly cerebral. In truth, it is somewhat lower. This is "gut feeling" territory, and the Bible is on target when it identifies the seat of our emotions—especially involving religion—in the messy area of the bowels. I, for one—if you can cope with the picture—have occasionally let my "guts" rule my head. The odd pungent article or "Letter to the Editor" has been rattled off only to make me wonder later on if Jesus would have phrased it in quite the same way. I have my doubts.

And now, I cannot do it. I have met those with whom I disagree. I have seen them as people, as fellow Christians, and I've had to stop demonizing them. Simple as that. On both sides, there are dedicated and honest people of God, all largely motivated by the defense of God's Word and the presentation of a credible Good News. I can no longer doubt their integrity and calmly write off my brothers and sisters as the enemy. There has to be another way.

We could spend the rest of our book detailing how Christians on both sides of the debate have been hurt, how they have had to defend themselves. For me, the space is best used laying out the various approaches to Genesis in as balanced a manner as possible, and even making each of the arguments as strong as it could possibly be.

After doing this, I will draw some conclusions. Hopefully, these will move us toward a Christian counterculture—extracting the good and the honest from all available arguments.

Chapter 15

God Using Evolution

Earlier, we noted a survey of leading Anglican evangelicals at their annual assembly. The large majority believed in an old earth and God-directed evolution, and here's what they made of Genesis 1:

- ❖ "A presentation designed to teach a religious lesson."

- ❖ "Partly historical + divinely supernatural."

- ❖ "Typology."

- ❖ "Partly historical, not just a myth."

- ❖ "Pictorial representation of the truth that universal and human history begins with God's creation."

❖ "Poetic/symbolic presentation designed to teach God's role and purpose."

❖ "An inspired theological reflection on creation—the why, not the how, being central."

❖ "Spiritually historical—some moment in time when pre-man physically was constituted 'man' in God's image."

❖ "An extended anthropomorphism—God seen as man working a seven-day week."

❖ "Special genre that shows the creation of the kingdom of God before the Fall ... not science or history but an inspired statement about the way the world was before the Fall."

❖ "Explanation of creation ... attributing it to God—I don't think the timescales are particularly important."

❖ "The creation narrative ... to establish who rather than how. ... God's work is orderly and patterned. A Big Bang probably happened ... evolution following it."

We could note the following from this:

1. A variety of views on the start of Genesis, and a new freedom to express them.

2. At the center is a core agreement: Genesis is a picture that needs to be interpreted.

3. There are familiar echoes from the leading evangelical Bible commentators and teachers of the last two generations.

It is to these influential commentators that we now turn. The majority of commentators accept that God has used evolution and see early Genesis as written not for a scientific age but for a pre-science people. They adopt the basic questions of biblical interpretation. How would the first audience/readers have understood Genesis 1? What did the author want to tell them? What was the context (the community circumstances) in which it was written? What type of language is used—history, poetry, or something special?

JOHN H. WALTON

This past Professor of Old Testament at Moody Bible Institute, now teaching at Wheaton Graduate School, believes that modern science has affected our view of the past. As a result, when we look at the Bible "we no longer realize we are asking the wrong questions." He explains:

> It only distorts the biblical text to try to read science between the lines, as if the text were constructed to accommodate modern scientific understanding. Nevertheless, it also undermines the text to reduce it to a harmless variation of primitive mythological misconceptions.

BRUCE K. WALTKE

This Professor of Old Testament at the Reformed Theological Seminary, and Professor Emeritus of Biblical Studies at Regent

College, is one of the leading evangelical Old Testament scholars. In his 2001 commentary on Genesis, he gives the four reasons why he believes the creation account and science should
not be confused.

First, he insists, Genesis and science discuss essentially different matters.

> The subject ... is God, not the forces of nature.
> The transcendent God is a subject that science
> cannot discuss.

Second, he notes that the language of Genesis and science is
entirely different. The creation account is formed in everyday
speech

> ... rather than mathematics and technical termi-
> nology. ... The intent ... is not to specify the
> geological and genetic methods of creation, but
> to definitively establish that creation is a result
> of God's creative acts.

Third, the purposes of Genesis and science also differ.

> Genesis is prescriptive, answering the questions
> of who and why and what ought to be, whereas
> the purpose of science is to be descriptive,
> answering the questions of what and how ...
> [it] is not particularly concerned with the ques-
> tions a scientist asks; rather, it wants to provide
> answers to the questions science cannot

answer—who has created this world and for
what purpose?

Fourth, since they are addressed to different types of communi-
ties, Genesis and science require distinct means for validation.

> Science ... requires empirical testing for valida-
> tion. Genesis, addressed to the covenant commu-
> nity of God, requires the validation of the
> witness of the Spirit to the heart (Romans 8:16).
> For these reasons, the Genesis creation account
> cannot be delineated as a scientific text.[1]

JOHN STEK

This former fellow of the Calvin Center for Christian
Scholarship believes that the author of Genesis had no interest
in or awareness of cosmic and evolutionary issues.

> His concerns were exclusively religious. His
> intent was to proclaim knowledge of the true
> God as he manifested himself in his creative
> works, to proclaim a right understanding of
> humankind, the world, and history that knowl-
> edge of the true God entails—and to proclaim
> the truth concerning these matters in the face of
> the false religious notions dominant throughout
> the world of his day.[2]

BILLY GRAHAM

The famous evangelist always left open the issue of how God created, but he did not rule out evolution, writes television presenter David Frost, who interviewed him on his British visits. He quotes Dr. Graham:

> I don't think that there's any conflict at all between science today and the Scriptures. I think that we have misinterpreted the Scriptures many times and we've tried to make the Scriptures say things they weren't meant to say. I think that we have made a mistake by thinking the Bible is a scientific book. The Bible is not a book of science. The Bible is a book of Redemption, and of course I accept the Creation story. I believe that God did create the universe. I believe that God created man, and whether it came by an evolutionary process and at a certain point he took this person or being and made him a living soul or not, does not change the fact that God did create man … whichever way God did it makes no difference as to what man is and man's relationship to God.[3]

J. I. PACKER

Jim Packer, part of the backbone of British biblical studies since the last half of the twentieth century, also believed that "Scripture was given to reveal God, not to address scientific issues in scientific terms."[4]

Dr. Packer, Professor of Historical and Systematic Theology at Regent College, Vancouver, added elsewhere,

> I believe in the inerrancy of Scripture, and main-
> tain it in print, but I cannot see that anything ...
> in the first chapters of Genesis or elsewhere,
> bears on the biological theory of evolution one
> way or the other. On the theory itself, as a non-
> scientist, watching from a distance the disputes
> of experts, I suspend judgement.[5]

GORDON WENHAM

This theologian and Senior Lecturer in Religious Studies at the College of St. Paul and St. Mary in Cheltenham mourns the over-literalistic interpretations leading to the clash between science and religion.

> It has been unfortunate that one device that our
> narrative uses to express the coherence and pur-
> posiveness of the creator's work, namely, the
> distribution of the various creative acts to six
> days, has been seized on and interpreted over-
> literalistically, with the result that science and
> Scripture have been pitted against each other
> instead of being seen as complementary.
> Properly understood, Genesis justifies the scien-
> tific experience of unity and order in nature. The
> six-day schema is but one of several means
> employed in this chapter to stress the system and

order that has been built into creation. Other
devices include the use of repeating formulae,
the tendency to group words and phrases into
tens and sevens ... the arrangement of creative
acts into matching groups, and so on.[6]

NICK MERCER

The above groups and patterns were picked up by former
London Bible College tutor Nick Mercer when addressing a
Spring Harvest conference audience on science and religion. It
was one of the reasons, he explained, why Genesis had been
given to a violent and capricious age of plagues, infant deaths,
famine, and earthquake.

Genesis 1 is arguing that there is order in the
cosmos ... the structure of Genesis 1 itself is ...
to establish that order. You can see lots of patterns ... that shows something of that order. I'm
not into Bible numerology in a big way but
even I couldn't get round some of the numbers
that occur, especially sevens, tens and threes.
Genesis 1:1 has seven Hebrew words in it. Verse
two has two times seven. The seventh paragraph
(chapter 2:1–3) has five times seven words in it.
The total six days have 59 sevens, and the
whole passage is three times three times seven
times seven. For the ancient man, numbers had
great significance ... this is establishing that the
universe is a well-ordered universe.

Sounds odd, I know, but it works in the Hebrew. Nick Mercer added three other reasons why commentators believe that Genesis 1 is a tract addressing the times in which it was written.

> One of the issues was monotheism versus polytheism; was there just one God ... or were there many gods? Deuteronomy 4:19 deals with the background. "When you look up to the sky ... do not be enticed into bowing down to them." And that's why ... arguably, Moses or whoever wrote it, didn't use the normal Hebrew words for sun and moon ... because they were the same for the Babylonian sun gods.
>
> And therefore he used the words for Greater light ... Lesser light. Also, there was the status of men and women and the gods ... the Bible was anxious to make it clear that every man and woman (women being included was quite revolutionary for those times) was made in God's image. Not just kings and pharaohs and the elect of society.
>
> A fourth reason is that God is God over all. The myths circulating at the time show that man was seen as being made out of the gods' entrails or spittle or even their excreta. There were struggles going on in the universe and man was a result of all these struggles. Genesis 1 is majestic. There is no struggle. God speaks and it is so. It happens.[7]

For all the above reasons, theistic evolutionists want to accept early Genesis as a picture of creation open to interpretation. They do this for three reasons:

1. The book of God's works has, they believe, educated their interpretation of the first part of the book of God's words. It is similar to Galileo's discovery, which put a new slant on our view of the earth.

2. Genesis is to be understood in the light of modern science, for the sake of the Gospel and its credibility.

3. Modern biblical criticism has helped by giving rules governing interpretation, such as answering the important questions concerning the context in which it was written.

The last words go to Bruce Waltke. He writes that the Christian message is "hindered by a continued adherence to the ... principle that valid scientific theories must be consistent with a woodenly literal reading of Genesis."[8] He insists that "attempts to harmonize Genesis with science" have led to "implausible interpretations of Genesis 1 ... presupposing a young earth and denying evolution."

He concludes, "Let each book speak its own language and be appropriately exegeted and exposited [explained], and let each in its own way bring praise to the Creator, the God and Father of our Lord Jesus Christ."

It is to what Waltke terms "implausible interpretations" of Genesis that we now turn in our next chapter. Not that they were at all "implausible" to those who proposed them, though some

have fallen into disuse. In the last 150 years, ingenious commentators have tried many ways to harmonize Genesis 1 and
modern science. Come and see.

NOTES:

1. Bruce K. Waltke, *Genesis: A Commentary* (Zondervan, 2001).

2. J. Stek, "What Says the Scripture," in *Portraits of Creation* (Eerdmans, 1990).

3. Quoted in David Frost, *Billy Graham: Personal Thoughts of Public Man* (Lion, 1997).

4. J. I. Packer, *God Has Spoken* (Hodder & Stoughton, 1988).

5. J. I. Packer, *The Evangelical Anglican Identity Problem* (Intervarsity Press, 1978).

6. Gordon J. Wenham, *Word Biblical Commentary, Volume 1, Genesis 1–15* (Word, 1987).

7. Nick Mercer, "The Bible & Science: Friends or Foes?" Spring Harvest tape (BS36 Optional Seminar 36), 1988.

8. Bruce K. Waltke, "The Literary Genre of Genesis, Chapter One," *Crux* 27 no. 4, (1991): 2–10.

Chapter 16

Balancing the Books

The fossils were there. The earth really did look ancient. Evolution was a growing force. Near-humans had lived on their private caving estates. And now people were beginning to laugh at the quaint Genesis version of creation. What was a thinking and sensitive Christian to do?

Not everybody, of course, could easily transfer early Genesis from the history department to poetry. Some were desperate enough at the beginning to entertain anything that would salvage the Scriptures from what appeared to be the ravages of modern science.

Numerous solutions surfaced as commentators and scholars sought a concord or balance between the two—earning the description of concordists. One of the very first came even

while Charles Darwin's quill was scribbling away at his mechanism for evolution.

THE GAP THEORY

Renowned Scottish theologian Thomas Chalmers introduced
this theory in the wake of Hutton's startling new geology. It
also came a few months after William Smith emerged from his
canal trenches to print his underground snapshot of island
geology in 1815.

Thomas Chalmers was an incredible Christian force, open-
ing 216 churches in one six-year period. He was the first
Moderator of the Free Church Assembly after the Disruption,
the breakaway of 474 ministers from the Church of Scotland.
He enjoyed his professorship in theology in New College,
Edinburgh, and died over a decade before Darwin's *On the
Origin of Species* came out.

He was so concerned about the reputation of his beloved
Scriptures in the light of the new geology that he proposed a
gap between the first two verses of Genesis 1, as we noted earlier. Into this huge gap of millions of years, he believed every
geological age and fossil could safely be placed. It was later
made famous worldwide by its inclusion in the 1909 Scofield
Reference Bible.

The idea matured through George H. Pember in his book
Earth's Earliest Ages, and also through Weston W. Field's
book *Unformed and Unfilled.* Others added bits and pieces,
and the full-blown theory saw God's first creation coming to
grief, largely at the hands of heaven's leading light, Lucifer.

Pre-Adamic races populated the earth, and God's right-hand angel fancied his chances. This was where Lucifer tripped and ended up as Satan.

Into Lucifer's gap went the T-Rex and his fellow dinosaurs of the Jurassic period. Had the gap still been credible today, it could comfortably have taken Homo habilis, Homo erectus, and anything else that was unearthed. Others, like Weston Field, suggested that this was all wiped out in Lucifer's flood, producing the formless and dark void out of which arose God's re-creation (in Genesis 1:2).

The popular appeal of this theory was huge. Into one simple gap, all the biblical problems that faced the nineteenth-century church could be dumped. Any Bible challengers for generations to come could simply be stilled by directing them to the Gap Theory.

However, the gap failed the test of time and began to lose support when conflicts with other parts of the Bible arose. The difficulties began to outweigh the merits:

❖ Lucifer's flood was pure speculation.

❖ Death and sin were supposed to have come in through Adam (see Romans 5:12). How then could there have been such mayhem beforehand?

❖ Blood was shed from the foundation of the world, but the foundation was recognized as Adam's time (see Luke 11:50–51).

Today, the gap theory has gone the way of the dinosaurs for Bible commentators, though a fifth of those who answered the

Anglican Evangelical Conference survey checked off their liking for the idea.

THOUSAND-YEAR DAY THEORY

"But do not forget this one thing, dear friends: With the Lord a day is like a thousand years, and a thousand years are like a day" (2 Peter 3:8).

"For a thousand years in your sight are like a day that has just gone by, or like a watch in the night" (Psalm 90:4).

Many came to understand that these texts gave them license to interpret "day" in Genesis 1 (*yom* in the Hebrew) as a long period of time. The "thousand years" were obviously symbolic in the above texts. Why not likewise in Genesis? Again, it seemed the answer to all those problem fossils and geological strata.

Others felt that the texts and "day" were being wrenched out of their context. The creationists, for example, gave time, money, and paper to defend y*om* as a literal twenty-four hours. They believed the following:

❖ The contexts of Psalm 90 and 2 Peter were vastly different from that of Genesis.

❖ *Yom,* when used elsewhere in the Bible, meant a twenty-four-hour day.[1]

❖ It meant twenty-four hours in the Ten Commandments,

which supported a twenty-four-hour-day sequence. The use of it in the commandments made some uneasy. Reinterpreting Genesis was one thing, but rewriting the commandments was a step too far.

❖ If plants were created on the third "day" and bees not until the fifth, how would the plants have survived if "day" meant a long geological epoch?

As for theistic evolutionists, they were, meanwhile, tiring of the day/*yom* argument and felt more comfortable treating the whole first chapter of Genesis as a picture or symbol, rather than relying on word games.

THE REVELATORY DAY THEORY

Moses took it all in, dipped his quill, and began to scribe, "And there was evening and there was morning—the first day." Then he did the same thing on subsequent days as God revealed the rest of His creation. This is known as the revelatory day theory. According to this, Genesis 1 is not about creation days, but about the days on which God showed Moses what He had done.

This attracted support from 15 percent in the Anglican evangelicals surveyed, but one theologian among them dismissed it with the words, "It violates the *sensus plenor* [the obvious and main meaning of the text], and a passage is not handled that way elsewhere in the Bible."

It seemed a fair point. He said the same about the revelatory device theory. This involved the author of Genesis using the days as a way of organizing his material. Nobody else liked this much, either.

FRAMEWORK HYPOTHESIS

This was developed in the late 1930s. It sees the whole week as a literary device. The author has used this as a framework to get over the message of an orderly God who works and rests (six days plus one). The author then takes the days to be real, literal twenty-four-hour periods, days that actually happened.

We could go on with more theories. But now to the creationist view of Genesis ...

NOTE:

1. Whenever *yom* is used with a numeral it is a literal twenty-four hours, as in Nehemiah 6:15 recording that it took 52 days to finish the walls of Jerusalem (see also Malcolm Bowden's "Pamphlet 328" of the Creation Science Movement, 2000).

Chapter 17

The Case for Creationism

Creationists form a protest movement. The creation societies and members are reacting against the Church, as they see it, watering down God's Word to suit mistaken science. The main group in Britain for many years was called the Evolution Protest Movement, as we noted earlier.

Creationists begin with the "Book of God's Words," and everything from anthropology to zoology, including geology, must be seen through Scripture-tinted glasses. Anything that is unclear and out of focus is not Scripture's fault. The problem lies with the shortcomings of what is being viewed. This is the master key to unlock the interior of creationism, as Dr. John Peet, writing for the Creation Science Movement, underlines.

The Scriptures are inerrant. The rejection of biblical creation has led to the evangelical dispute on the infallibility (true in matters of faith)/inerrancy (true in matters of fact) issue. The Scriptures are our supreme authority. The evangelist's cry, "Bible says" has been replaced by "science says."

> **Creationists begin with the "Book of God's Words," and everything from anthropology to zoology, including geology, must be seen through Scripture-tinted glasses.**

Having surrendered to the skeptics re-origins, there has been a general weakening on the authority of Scripture on other issues. If we can rewrite Genesis 1 to 11, we can do the same elsewhere.[1]

They fight for Genesis 1–11 because the majority of theologians have for a century regarded it as not literal or historical.

Of course, this is a highly sensitive and painful area for all, especially for those among theistic evolutionists who regard themselves as Bible-first Christians. All sides believe they are rescuing the Scriptures and the Gospel and making them credible to a needy world. Despite obvious reverence and integrity for Scripture on all sides, each accuses the others of betrayal.

The creationists insist that the blame for the loss of Scripture's reputation lies at the Church's door because it has surrendered. They quote Darwin's first "PR man," Thomas Huxley:

> Christian theology must stand or fall with the historical trustworthiness of the Jewish Scriptures. The very conception of the Messiah, or Christ, is inextricably interwoven with Jewish history ... the Hebrew Scriptures have no evidential value unless they possess the historical character assigned to them.[2]

All sides believe they are rescuing the Scriptures and the Gospel and making them credible to a needy world.

Today's scientists are just as scathing. Professor Steve Jones said during a BBC Nick Ross phone-in on science and religion: "Throughout history, religion has all along tried to stop scientific progress. What it's now doing is retreating so far back in its claims that it's got almost nothing left."[3]

Leading atheist author Philip Pullman in *The Amber Spyglass* has Mary Malone telling Lyra and Will that the

Christian religion is a very powerfully convincing mistake: "It doesn't gel at all with the more convincing account that is given by Darwinian evolution—and the scientific account is far more persuasive intellectually. Far more persuasive."[4]

> The creationists believe the Church has too easily surrendered to a myth.

Explaining how he was brought up as an Anglican but lost his faith, Philip Pullman gave this as one reason: "It began to seem impossible to reconcile the creation story with the scientific account."[5]

Theistic evolutionists would claim at this point that the Pullmans of this world would have been saved by their harmonization of Genesis and science. The creationists believe the Church has too easily surrendered to a myth. They quote Søren Lovtrup in his book *Darwinism: The Refutation of a Myth:*

> I suppose that nobody will deny that it is a great misfortune if an entire branch of science becomes addicted to a false theory. But this is what has happened in biology. ... I believe one day the Darwin myth will be ranked the greatest deceit in the history of science.[6]

Creationists refuse to bow before a scientific myth. Treating Genesis 1–11 as less than literal is impossible for creationists for several reasons. For instance:

Why didn't God just say he had evolved everything? The

creationists believe it would have been easier for God to tell the first humans that he had promoted a couple of their ape cousins and reformed them in His image. Why inspire a story that would eventually be laughed at, causing belief in Himself to be decimated?

WHAT ABOUT THE BIBLE PEOPLE?

Creationists ask why God allowed everybody in the Bible, including His Son Jesus Christ, to treat early Genesis as literally true if it wasn't?

JESUS

- ❖ Matthew 19:4: "Haven't you read … that at the beginning the Creator 'made them male and female?'" (Creationists say that "at the beginning" does not mean after 15 billion years and various "homo" species.)

- ❖ Matthew 23:35: "Blood that has been shed on earth, from the blood of righteous Abel." (Jesus saw Abel as a real person.)

- ❖ Luke 17:26–27: Jesus also took Noah and the Flood as historical. Creationists also note that the Flood destroyed "all" mankind.

ISAIAH

- ❖ Isaiah 2:22: "Man, who has but a breath in his nostrils." Also 42:5, "Gives breath to its people."

- ❖ Isaiah 45:12: "It is I who … created [bara] mankind."

(*Bara* is the word used for "created afresh," not from some existing species, say creationists.)

PAUL

❖ 1 Corinthians 15:22: "For as in Adam all die, so in Christ all will be made alive." (In one sentence, Christ cannot be real while Adam is not, insist creationists.)

❖ Romans 5:14: "Death reigned from the time of Adam." (Not from before, with the loss of the weakest, creationists claim.)

❖ 1 Timothy 2:13: "For Adam was formed first, then Eve." Paul accepted early Genesis as real. He would have been surprised to hear Christians saying that they were created together, as God breathed his image into two prehumans.

❖ Luke 3, plus the genealogies in Genesis 5 and 11 and 1 Chronicles 1, all treat Adam as historical.

Why would God let so many important people believe this if Adam and Eve weren't real? Why allow people to base the New Testament on something that did not happen? Why let it go on for millennia right up to the nineteenth century? These questions cause creationists genuine concern.

WHY DID GOD TAKE SO LONG?

Creationists understand that some fellow Christians are impressed at a God who would take billions of years over his creation. But the creationists themselves have difficulty envisioning it. They are not convinced with the following approximate time scale.

15 BILLION YEARS AGO

God creates. His aim is to produce a creature in His image. The project is launched with a Big Bang (or something). The Almighty then uses 10 billion years guiding the resultant bits and pieces into a universe. This is how long it takes stars to form the heavier, life-supporting elements like carbon (see appendix on the universe).

4.4 BILLION YEARS AGO

His Spirit broods over one of the smaller bits of debris, which He plans to develop and populate. It takes millions of years to slow down and cool and for the remaining necessary elements, chemicals, and forces to form.

4 BILLION YEARS AGO

A few million years are needed to arrange a life-making mix of chemicals (via a stagnant pond, or hot undersea geysers, or in crystals of increasing complexity, or suspended in droplets of water at high altitude, or even importing the seed of life from outer space—see chapter 8).

3.5 BILLION YEARS AGO

Planets, stars, particles, and matter now in place, the Creator turns to the microscopic. Divine astronomer becomes microbiologist, creating amino acids or proteins, or DNA, or RNA, or something simpler. (Again, go back to chapter 8.)

3 BILLION YEARS AGO

The Creator builds selection and imperfection into the system. DNA, the blueprint of life at the center of all cells, is allowed to mutate at set rates. Minimutations battle with harsh environments (lack of food, difficult temperatures, overpopulation, and so on) to ensure that the weakest are put down.

6 MILLION YEARS AGO

The weak continue to die off over three billion years as God develops life. Then He is ready to mold His pinnacle of creation, progressing through a bent-over, low-slung, two-legged, big-brained ape. Once straightened out and up, He can remodel the creature internally to be like Himself.

150,000 YEARS AGO

Homo sapiens are made. But still God waits. A few thousand years ago, He eventually selected a couple of shorn descendants. Both were deprogramed, altering 1.5 percent of their genes, the difference between humans and their nearest ancestor.

WHAT OF THE GREAT COMMUNICATOR?

The Scriptures, say creationists, reveal a God who loves to communicate in down-to-earth language. The original humans fall out with their Maker. He then makes His plans crystal clear through angels, prophets, writers, miracles, and judgments. Not content with go-betweens, He finally comes back in the flesh of His Son. He spends three years teaching with signs and wonders and then leaves his Holy Spirit with each Christian so that they might go on being amazed.

> Many Christian doctrines are rooted in the early chapters of Genesis. If they are not an accurate portrayal of origins, our Christian doctrines are built on an unstable foundation.

The creationists now ask why a God who has spoken so plainly should use an Adam and Eve "fairy story" on which to base the description of His creation. Not only does it give a false, misleading doctrine of Scripture, they say, but it also affects the following.

A CONTINUING NEED FOR GOD

Albert Einstein is reputed to have once said, "I believe in God, but I have to confess that there's nothing left for Him to do." He retreats to being the celebrity who switched it all on. Dr. Peet writes for the Christian Science Movement:

> Many Christian doctrines are rooted in the early chapters of Genesis. If they are not an accurate portrayal of origins, our Christian doctrines are built on an unstable foundation. The God of the Genesis account is sovereign. Genesis 1 has over 30 references to an active controlling God. Evolution dethrones God, making Him unnecessary and impotent.[7]

The Creator looked at each stage and said, "It is good." After making humanity, He said, "It is very good." Dr. Peet writes:

> Goodness implies beauty, fitness and design. Evolutionary processes involve disaster, death, extinction, earthquakes, asteroids etc. ... on a huge and bloody scale. In short, evolution requires death; but death is an enemy (see Genesis 3:19, John 11 and 1 Corinthians 15:26).[8]

This point is especially relevant when we consider our population poser of chapter 4. According to anthropology and evolutionary theory, near-humans have lived for 150,000 years. They reckon that four billion of them died, most of them in terrifying ways. They were regularly wiped out by starvation, plague, pestilence, or horrific catastrophes. If near-humans were not being annihilated by meteorites, then volcanoes were frying them alive. This must have happened, because otherwise the population would have overrun the earth.

Now, I'm using this emotive language because the creationists do. Their point is this: Did God set all this in motion and still instruct the storywriter of Genesis to declare it was all "good"? And if this is true, and all this mayhem is "good," what does that make God?

Atheistic and even theistic evolutionists argue that all this had to happen out of necessity. This was the only way life could happen. It is neither good nor bad. It is amoral. The creationists argue that such a bloodthirsty system of creation makes God more like the devil. They are much happier with the Garden of Eden perfection, which then went wrong because of humanity's sin.

HUMAN STATUS

Creationists suggest that we should not be too surprised if men, women,

> Creationists suggest that we should not be too surprised if men, women, and children behave like animals if we teach them that they come from animals.

and children behave like animals if we teach them that they come from animals. Dr. Peet suggests that man gets much of his dignity from Genesis. Life is precious (see Genesis 4:10–11; 9:6), so much so that there is salvation from the consequences of the Fall (see Genesis 3:15). He is to have a Sabbath rest (see Genesis 2:1–2). The basis of marriage and sexual relationships is in Adam and Eve (see Genesis 1:27–28; 2:18; 3:16), as is the work ethic and responsibility to God as stewards of the earth (see Genesis 1:28; 2:1–2). The Fall in Genesis 3 and God's judgment are both central to the later salvation made possible in Jesus Christ. All this and much more, claim the creationists, is under threat when Genesis 1–11 is not treated properly. They acknowledge that the devil misleads humanity and believe that it is no coincidence that Genesis should have been undermined.

> Professor Hamblin points out that scientists are, of course, no less and no more prone to human frailties than any others, but they have had their darker moments.

WHY NOT HISTORY?

Dr. Andrew McIntosh in his book *Genesis for Today* quotes "a number of experts" who disagree that literary analysis demotes Genesis 1–11 to myth.

> These chapters cannot be identified as non-
> historical on the basis of any generally appli-
> cable literary criteria. Neither are they
> distinguishable from Genesis 12 to 50 by sig-
> nificant differences in their literary character.
> There is no great divide between Genesis 11
> and Genesis 12. In fact Genesis 11 interlocks
> with the preceding and following narratives.[9]

And, asks McIntosh, if everything before Genesis 12 is myth, why are Cain and Abel treated as historical in Hebrews 11:14 and 12:4? This is also true of 1 John 3:12 and Jude 11.

ON WHOSE AUTHORITY?

We give the last word on creationism to Professor Terry Hamblin. He took time away from his discipline (hematology) to contrast the authority of scientists and of Scripture in a Portsmouth talk, later published by the Christian Science Movement.[10]

Professor Hamblin points out that scientists are, of course, no less and no more prone to human frailties than any others, but they have had their darker moments. The professor takes us around a rogues' gallery of scientists who cheated to support their theories.

❖ Ernst Haeckel thought human evolution was rerun in the womb, so he altered pictures of embryos to fit his wrong theory.

❖ The scientists responsible for the phony missing links like Piltdown, Peking, Nebraska, and Java man (see chapter 11).

❖ Those responsible for false scientific papers; results doctored to fit theories; fraud over AIDS; skin grafts and transgenic mice; faking heart data; passing monkey cells off as human; and anthropological shenanigans.

"The success of Darwinism was accompanied by a decline in scientific integrity," a professor wrote in the introduction to an edition of Darwin's *On the Origin of Species*.[11] Professor Hamblin adds, "Scientists are fallen humans like the rest of us, and are not infallible. Where then do we turn to for true authority?"

His answer, of course, is that we turn to Scripture—Jesus Christ. He lists the texts we have already noted regarding creation and evolution, quoting heavily from the letters of the apostle Paul, and concludes:

> Some will object further "Yes, but that's Paul.
> We only believe what Jesus said." Matthew
> 19:4 records that Christ said, "Have you not
> read that he which made them at the beginning
> made them male and female ... one flesh?"
> referring to Genesis 1:27 with 2:24.

So our ultimate authority is Jesus Christ, through whom God made the worlds, being the brightness of His glory and the express image of His person, who lends His authority to the Genesis account of the creation of all things.

CONCLUSION

The creationists believe that a God who loves to communicate plainly did so, literally, from the beginning of the Bible onward. They discount:

- ❖ stories that mislead God's Son and every other key leader for 4,000 years up to the nineteenth and twentieth centuries;

- ❖ a God who kills off the weakest and thinks it is "very good";

- ❖ humans developing from apes;

- ❖ a deity more or less locked out of His own universe by necessity while it develops over billions of years;

- ❖ one who must work through the laws as we know them today;

- ❖ undermining the basis of most Christian doctrine as found in Genesis;

- ❖ scientists whom they see as imperfect, as is the rest of humanity.

Such is the core of the case for creation. Again, you must judge.

NOTES:

1. Dr. J. H. John Peet, Pamphlet 335 (Creation Science Movement, July 2001), 2.

2. T. H. Huxley, *Science and Hebrew Tradition* (Macmillan, 1893).

3. Steve Jones, "Science and Religion, Nick Ross Phone-in," BBC Radio, April 4, 2000.

4. Philip Pullman interview in *Third Way* (April 2002): 23.

5. Ibid., 24.

6. Søren Lovtrup, *Darwinism: The Refutation of a Myth* (Croom Helm, 1987), 422.

7. As note 1, p. 1.

8. Ibid., 2.

9. D. Guthrie, J. A. Motyer, A. M. Stibbs, D. J. Wiseman eds., N*ew Bible Commentary, Revised* (InterVarsity Press), 80; M. D. Kline, *Genesis: Historicity and Literary Parallels, 1967*. Quoted in Dr. Andrew McIntosh, *Genesis for Today* (DayOne, 1997), 35.

10. Professor Terry Hamblin, "On Whose Authority?" Pamphlet 298 (Creation Science Movement, 1995).

11. Ibid., 3. Quoting the introduction to the 1956 edition of Charles Darwin's *On the Origin of Species.*

Chapter 18

Summing Up

Presuming you are not one of those back-of-the-book "peep-ers," congratulations on reaching this last chapter. We thought of awarding a survival-of-the-fittest medal, but decided that might not be entirely appropriate.

Words like "faultless" and "flawless" are not normally associated with our species. Something went wrong with the prototype. And not only is there our original sin to consider but also the massive scope of our subject. Could anybody be entirely perfect in every area where we have been? I therefore suggest ...

HUMILITY

In Christianity, devoted and committed people of God cannot agree about Genesis. Yet all fight for the integrity of Scripture and the Gospel of Jesus Christ. We tread carefully because of our mistakes in the past. Poor interpretation has led some to support slavery, or apartheid, or even an earth-centered universe.

In science, highly motivated and respected professors have crossed swords, and only a fool would risk getting in the way. This stated, humility is also needed in science because of its past errors. After all, our scientific knowledge has been wrong more than it has been right. Some of yesterday's watertight theories look decidedly leaky today. For example:

> **We tread carefully because of our mistakes in the past. Poor interpretation has led some to support slavery, or apartheid, or even an earth-centered universe.**

❖ The oscillating age of the earth and universe (the earth was embarrassingly older than the universe for some years pre-World War II).

❖ Thalidomide, bloodsucking leeches to cure all ailments, classifying criminals by reading bumps on human heads.

❖ Smoking is good for your image and health.

❖ Heavier-than-air machines can't fly.

❖ No human can travel faster than 30 mph and survive (up
to Stephenson's Rocket) ... travel faster than the speed
of sound and survive (up to the 1950s) ... travel in space
and survive (up to the 1960s).

Of course, we progress through our mistakes, as thalidomide and leeches demonstrate in their controlled uses today,
and each generation should remember that what is gospel in science today may be heresy tomorrow and what is heresy today
may bear elements of truth. Humility, then, is useful, but we
still have to reach a verdict. By this time, you might want to
throw up your hands and pronounce "a curse on all your
houses"! Yet God requires that we subdue and manage. That's
our job (see Genesis 1:28).

FUNDAMENTALISM

What people accept is often related to their starting point.

❖ The Darwinian fundamentalist, who finds it hard to let
god have a capital letter, will want to worship only
Evolution and Survival of the Fittest.

❖ The Christian fundamentalist will often wear divine
blinkers and assign evolution and science to hell.

❖ Liberal fundamentalists will demand the death sentence
for fundamentalism, except their own brand.

There is a fundamentalist in each of us. Here essential, primary non-negotiables reign. The arguments of our book will hopefully highlight for us the …

ESSENTIALS

"Stand up for the essentials," wrote Liverpool's first bishop, J. C. Ryle. "Stand down on inessentials." I offer the following for your consideration.

We are the body of Christ. I must not amputate those who disagree with my infallible interpretation of the Book. The essential is to treat it—literally or literary—as God's Word.

> We are the body of Christ. I must not amputate those who disagree with my infallible interpretation of the Book. The essential is to treat it—literally or literary—as God's Word.

Among the minimum essentials for Christians will be:

❖ a Creator;

❖ a real Adam and Eve;

❖ a beginning that was "good";

❖ a Fall that wasn't;

❖ the promise of a Savior.

To be sure, we can argue the niceties of these and others, but as we do, perhaps we need to relegate to our second division one unhelpful attribute—emotional attachment.

As I said at the beginning, I have held most positions regarding our subject in my three-score years. But for twenty-five years, I followed one view in particular, and I now have to confess that it was an affair of the heart. Part of the reason for writing is that others might be able to focus unemotionally on God's essentials. Some people are scientific by nature; some are more artsy; others lean to theology or Scripture, or a combination of all or some of these. To any one of them, or all of them, we can become emotionally attached. Emotion is good. But it might not be essential. And this must go equally for the Christians as much as the scientists, especially those with a tendency towards fundamentalism.

SCIENCE

I fell for science while trapped for hours a mile down a coal pit. As the workers dug one shaken *Coal News* reporter out, they kept me calm with a running commentary on the beauty of our surroundings. Equally, I fell for God after my life caved in and He dug me out.

Since then, I have enjoyed the same bewildering, delightful, exasperating lot of all believers—balancing the Book of God's Words with the one covering His works. Rejection of either is not an option. Putting one in competition against the other is likewise useless. God's truth comes from both. Difficulties arise not between Christianity and science, but between the misreading of God's book of words and poor interpretation of the book of God's works. If the two books ever seem to be in conflict, it will always be the reader who is dyslexic.

> Difficulties arise not between Christianity and science, but between the misreading of God's book of words and poor interpretation of the book of God's works. If the two books ever seem to be in conflict, it will always be the reader who is dyslexic.

CHANGE COMING?

When a theory generates too many arguments and anomalies, history teaches us that it may not be fit enough to survive. Ptolemy's earth-centered theory of the universe, as we noted earlier, eventually tumbled before the greater explanation of Galileo. What of the clouds of uncertainty gathering about the theory of evolution? Could a rewrite be on the cards in the next generation? Consider:

❖ Pure Darwinism lasted a hundred years.

❖ The last generation rewrote essential elements to produce neo-Darwinism.

❖ Now, radical scientists are increasingly saying that

the natural selection mechanism—survival of the fittest—just cannot cope with all the variety and complexity and apparent design of nature. This intelligent design is even more notable as we view the universe and its evolution.

Some think that it is almost certain that a radical scientist will come up soon with a rewrite of the theory, or, more likely, even present an entirely new idea for the coming generation. In that case, all the arguments we have rehearsed in this book will be redundant.

Meanwhile, we keep to the essentials. We are allowed to enjoy, even tussle gently, these inessential issues, but we are advised to avoid them if they take over our lives. Paul advised Timothy to avoid myths and endless genealogies: "These promote controversies rather than God's work" (1 Timothy 1:4).

LET GOD BE GOD

We humans don't like gaps in our knowledge. In our desperation, we fill them with anything and everything. The Greeks and Romans filled their gaps with a pantheon of gods, but increased knowledge squeezed them out soon enough. We face the same fate for God, if we dare to slot Him into our present-day areas of ignorance. God is the very ground of our being, says the apostle Paul. He is the Creator in whom we move and have our being. He is not a god of the gaps; no stopgap (see Acts 17:28). All that is visible speaks on the invisible deity (see Romans 1:20).

Creation and evolution are not evangelistic weapons. There is no way that anybody will fall for God through the arguments we have dealt with here.

William of Occam (also spelt Ockham) got a papal wrap over his fourteenth-century knuckles for saying what most accept today: that God and the central truths of Christianity cannot be proved by philosophical or natural reason. Only revelation will do that—and that's God's job.

KEEP IT SIMPLE

William Occam came up with one more worthy idea—Occam's Razor. In its pure form, it sounds like nothing: entities are not to be multiplied without necessity. Translated, it means that we should not accept an idea or theory that is more complicated than it needs to be. Go for the simplest.

A Christian's job in countering culture is perhaps to go on reminding people about a Creator who has done things in His way, in His time, and wants a loving relationship with what He has made. Now, that's simple!

❖ EVOLUTION OUT THERE

APPENDIX:

The Universe

As we have noted, all is not cut and dried concerning the evolution of earth and life. Huge questions hover. But what of the universe? We take for granted that it is billions of years old because we are told this so often. Who are we to differ when popular television and the media in general accept its antiquity without doubt? But should we? Are there serious questions about the universe as well? The short answer is yes. For the long answer, read on.

LAW AND DISORDER

How can order arise out of disorder on its own? Cosmologists still struggle to explain how a Big Bang has produced the beauty and design with which the Hubble space telescope regularly dazzles us. How can an astronomical explosion produce a precise and finely tuned universe?

The same disorder argument cascades down the various levels of evolution. How can our blue globe of beauty and complexity emerge on its own? How can it then produce sentient life, and so on? How can it do all this when everything around us is going in the opposite direction? All is running down, not up. Energy is being used up. Expansion of the universe will one day stop. Maybe. And then collapse. Possibly. The stars are burning up. Our sun will go red and then die.

> DNA, genes, and life wear out. Things break down into disorder. They do not build up into the incredible, the beautiful, and the complex.

Closer to home, we are all too aware of things running down. I look in the mirror and I'm wearing some old man's face. I've suddenly acquired my mother's jowls. And what time and life have done to my six-pack is nobody's business but my own.

This is the Second Law of Thermodynamics, to give it its posh title. Its alias is the law of entropy (disorder). Very crudely, this means that anything left to itself sooner or later becomes more disorderly. Cars rust. Hips and muscles sag. DNA, genes, and life wear out. Things break down into disorder. They do not build up into the incredible, the beautiful, and the complex.

How then has our universe, governed by such a law of entropy, produced you and me—examples of the most intricate beings in a most complex world? Both creationists and theistic evolutionists might like to jump in with their obvious answers at this stage, but others go on searching.

EVOLUTION OF THE UNIVERSE

In this area, we do have more answers. And even more questions. Here's some of what we think is certain:

- ❖ Traveling at the speed of light, you could travel across our galaxy, the Milky Way, in 100,000 years.

- ❖ Ours is but one of countless galaxies, each with billions of stars. Edwin Hubble showed this by identifying several pulsating stars called cepheid variables in galaxies like the nearest, Andromeda. By measuring the period of pulsation, the brightness of these cepheids could be measured. These were then compared to the pulses of other fainter cepheids, which showed that they existed far beyond local galaxies. Andromeda was first calculated to be 900,000 light years away, but it turned out that somebody had misread the cepheids, and it now stands at more than two million light years away.

- ❖ It was shown that the spectra of most galaxies shift towards the longer (or red) wavelengths and this indicated that they were traveling away from the Milky Way. The phenomenon is parallel to the apparent rise and fall in pitch of a passing train or motorbike. It's known as the Doppler effect.

❖ Hubble's law states that the farther away galaxies are, the faster they are traveling. This has given the impression of the universe being like an expanding balloon.

❖ The universe is fifteen billion years old. Or at least it was on the day of writing this sentence. Experts assure me that it will definitely not change now, beyond a few million years. But they've said that before, and I'm being cautious. The universe was once as low as two billion years old, which caused red faces for many because, at the time, the earth was calculated as being three billion years older. It has been as high as twenty billion years. Watch this space!

So, these are some of the things we know. We think. Don't rock the boat! Of course, we know enough to get us to the moon and back, and perhaps even to Mars. We know the many constants, the forces that keep this universe in place. Physics and mathematics have given us much, though even some of these and other areas are now being questioned. Take, for example, the following:

❖ Steady State theory. Sir Fred Hoyle (with Hermann Bondi and Thomas Gold) suggested that the universe will always be as we see it today, more or less. Everything may be expanding, but that is balanced by a steady creation of new matter. Thus, the receding galaxies are replaced by new galaxies ad infinitum.

The discovery of background radiation from a Big Bang and bright quasars billions of years away have put the Steady State theory in moth balls.

❖ Cold Dark Matter (CDM). This is said to make up the missing nine-tenths of the universe. It is so called because it does not emit light. It is said to be ten or more times greater than all the material we can see at present. This dark energy is thought to be a repulsive force driving the universal expansion. If verified, it could support current theories of the universe, but still nobody has detected it. Now cosmologists think it might not even exist, and if it doesn't, then our current theories need a total revision.[1]

❖ "Heresy—change the speed of light and you can rewrite the history of the universe"—so ran a 1999 *New Scientist* front page.[2] This is supposed to be one of the rock-solid constants on which many other theories are based. Dr. Joao Magueijo believes that "the speed of light was once much greater than it is today."[3] If the speed of light was faster in the past than now, then starlight would have got to us sooner and the universe might be judged to be much younger. Television's Equinox filled a program with experts wanting to change the speed of light to solve problems associated with the Big Bang.[4]

❖ The universe may be a much stranger place than we now believe, according to the latest as we go to press. Dr. John Webb of New South Wales University, Australia, states that light coming from distant quasars suggests a fundamental physical constant may have been decreasing slightly. "This has major implications for our understanding of physics. ... If this is correct, it will radically change our view of the universe."[5]

❖ Big Bang and make-believe? What happened in the split seconds after our explosive start? Learned men and women talk confidently of "gravity going into a perverse stage" and thankfully for us "100 million particles of matter for every 99,999,999 particles of anti-matter." The *Guardian,* after reporting this, stated, "Scientists talk cheerfully and with immense confidence about the first few thousandths of a second of time, but secretly most people believe they are making them up as they go along."[6]

❖ Merely a frolic. Maybe the Big Bang, you and I, and this book are merely mirages. This whole universe might simply be "a frolic of primal information and matter."[7] If you think there's not much sense in that, try this next one.

❖ Fractal universe. Everything we know about the cosmos might be wrong, declared a *New Scientist* front page.[8] According to a dissident group of astronomers, the universe is not as Einstein said, "a smooth, homogenous place." If they're right, "the foundations of cosmology could crumble to dust."

All this is not to suggest for a moment that we should jump into bed with every front-page theory of the *New Scientist.* But it does tell us what our lack of knowledge leads to. *Horizon,* the

New Scientist, and every other weekly science paper exist simply because we know next to nothing about what is out there.

Every new find brings a new theory, and it is an exciting and exhilarating time to be alive. However, it is not the best time to come to any firm conclusions about what's out there, no matter what "pop scientists" tell us on the television.

NOTES:

1. Michael Rowan-Robinson, *New Scientist* (June 2002): 39–40.

2. *New Scientist,* July 24, 1999.

3. *The Times,* April 5, 2000.

4. *Equinox,* April 17, 2000.

5. BBC News Online article, May 17, 2002.

6. *Guardian,* March 3, 1997.

7. *New Scientist,* January 30, 1999.

8. *New Scientist,* August 21, 1999.

Glossary

Algorithm comes from the surname of a Persian mathematician who proposed that all processes could be broken down into small, step-by-step calculations—a foolproof, right-every-time recipe. In the game of tic-tac-toe, for example, an algorithm would not only teach the rules, but also explain how to pick up a pen, what an "O" was, how to draw one in one square while an opponent made an "X" in another. It would explain the consequences of each move so that even a mindless machine (like a computer) could play the game. Evolution came from a mindless algorithm, say some. Others say life cries out for an almighty mind.

Amino acids are the ingredients to make the building blocks of life. Twenty of these acids—mixtures of carbon, nitrogen, oxygen, and hydrogen—are used to make the protein "machines" on the factory floor of our cells.

Anthropic (*anthropoi* is Greek for humankind) is the principle that this universe has the extremely fine-tuned conditions to produce and support life up to humanity.

Archaeopteryx. Not long after Darwin's *Origins* hit the bookshelves, this apparent cross between a reptile and a bird was found in a German quarry in rocks said to be 145 million years old. Creationists say that it is just one of those oddities, like the duck-billed platypus. It is a freak of nature exhibiting features of different classes but in no way transitional. Evolutionists embraced archaeopteryx with the desperation of an ancient prospector grasping at something yellow. The century-old debate goes on. Is archaeopteryx the real twenty-four-carat missing link, or is it simply a fool's fossil?

Australopithecus. This hominid group reigned from just over four million years ago, according to anthropologists. They were small ape beings, like Lucy, who shared Africa in later years with flat-faced man (Kenyananthropus platyops). The Homo group began as Lucy's genus faded. This, you understand, is how it is at the time of writing. Even as I write (July 2002), the human family tree is facing another major overhaul after the discovery in Chad of the seven-million-year-old Toumai (hope for life) skull. It is thought to combine the features of ape men with those of later hominids. According to creationists, this is the latest stage in keeping the public informed that they are just clever apes.

Background radiation is thought to be the "noise" left after the Big Bang.

Cambrian, the era named after ancient Wales where the oldest fossil-bearing rocks (570–500 million years ago) were first found. Creationists point out that life as we know it today appears suddenly in this brief period. Evolutionists insist that up until then, life had no "hard parts" to fossilize.

Carbon-14 (radiocarbon) is absorbed by living organisms. When the organism dies, 14C decays into its daughter isotope of Nitrogen-14, taking 5,730 years to lose half of its radioactivity.

Carboniferous era is said to be the time that great coal- and oil-bearing deposits were laid around 300 million years ago. It was named by Conybeare in 1822 from a Welsh stratum.

Catastrophism originally stated that earth and life formed through massive violent events, like Noah's Flood. This was overwhelmed by Lyell's idea that everything evolved at a uniform rate (uniformitarianism). Modern geology is a hybrid of both.

Cenozoic is the modern "recent life" era (the last 65 millions years).

Cepheids are pulsating stars used by Edwin Hubble to show the vastness of the universe.

Chance is the flip of a coin. There is no design about the coin landing heads, tails, or on its edge. It doesn't necessarily have to land a certain way. It is pure chance.

Clade comes from the Greek word *klados,* meaning branch or twig. In evolution-speak, it is a group of organisms on a branch of the bush of evolution. A clade includes the supposed nearest common ancestor from which the branch of organisms sprouted. The study of the whole "tree" of clades is called cladistics, a method used to suggest links between organisms.

Cold Dark Matter (CDM) is thought to be the nine-tenths of matter missing in the universe. CDM and its effects are needed to explain how the universe is as it is today.

Concordists try to harmonize a literal Genesis creation with the theories of modern science, for example by introducing a gap between the first two verses of Genesis to allow for the geological ages.

Continental drift suggests that there was once only one huge land mass (Rodinia, over 500 million years ago), This reformed into Pangaea (about 250 million years ago) made up of Eurasia, Laurentia, and Gondwanaland. These and smaller land masses "ping-ponged" into our present world with the speed of a snail at death's door.

Creationism/Creation science is populated with degree+ Christians who rewrite the theories of modern -ologies to show how blind, unguided evolution is "impossible." Their arguments center on missing fossil links, lack of time for evolution, and the difficulties of unguided natural selection producing complex life that looks designed.

Cretaceous is from the Latin for chalk, found in abundance in this era (136 to 65 million years ago), such as in the White Cliffs of Dover.

Cro-Magnon, a rock outcrop in France's Dordogne region where early-man skeletal remains were found in 1886. Cro-Magnon culture boasted jewelry, with tools in stone and bone, plus galleries of cave paintings.

Cryptozoic means "hidden life," the time before the obvious evidence of life after the Cambrian (the Phanerozoic).

Cytoskeleton. Imagine a road map of blue highways plus red and green routes. Now let your mind stretch the map into a 3-D model, and you have a close picture of the skeleton of one of our cells. The highways are minitubes of protein, much finer than a hair. The other roads are even smaller thread-like protein fibers and filaments that determine cell shape and tensile strength. They also provide the muscle power for movement.

Deism sees God as the "clockmaker" who has wound up the world and left it to run as designed. It suited rationalistic, enlightened humanity, which disliked a God who had to become flesh in His Son to save wayward mankind. Deists also reject a God who inspired Genesis and the rest of Scripture.

Devonian era ranged over 50 million years starting about 395 million years ago and, yes, you've guessed, it was named after an area of Devon, famed for its underground riches. Devonian-type rock is found worldwide with generous lodes of zinc, copper, and oil, as well as tin. It is also a rich source of iron ore.

DNA (deoxyribonucleic acid) is one of two nucleic acids, generally in the cell nuclei. It is a highly complicated molecule wound in a double "helter-skelter" helix shape. It makes up the cell's chromosomes, on the "arms" of which are the genes. As such, it is the instruction manual to reproduce, whatever its host. The second nucleic acid, RNA (ribonucleic acid), acts as the "messenger," taking instructions from the "blueprint" department to the cell's protein "machines." Many evolutionists believe that nucleic acids were the first to evolve when life was at its most basic. Creationists say that "nucleic acid" is to "basic" as "human brain" is to "abacus." See also note 3, chapter 8.

Doppler effect. Austrian physicist Doppler worked out that a constant sound had a higher pitch when it approached and a lower one when going away. The most famous example is the whistle of a train as it goes through a station. The theory extends to light waves. A luminous light, like a star, shifts towards the red end of the spectrum when going away from earth (Red Shift).

Entropy or disorder. This is the Second Law of Thermodynamics. Left to itself, order always becomes disorder. Never the other way around. Our everyday possessions wear out. Shiny new cars rust. Old bangers never become showroom models, unless there's a loving, creative fanatic on hand. Those who believe that order emerged from the disorder of a Big Bang (or whatever) call themselves creationists.

Eocene. An epoch in the second-most recent Tertiary era (65 to 2.5 million years ago).

Evolution is the theory that life developed, from species to species, over millions of years, by chance or by design.

Fundamentalism is applied to those who have a strict biblical and Protestant view of life. It can be applied to anybody who has fundamentals that determine what he thinks and how he lives. This is as true for science as much as for religion.

Genes are strands of nucleic acids directing how to make one or more of a creature's characteristics. See DNA.

Gondwanaland. See Continental drift above.

Half-life. See Carbon-14 above.

Homo erectus/habilis/sapiens. The hominine line is thought to

have split around 2.6 million years ago at least twice—homo and aus-
tralopithecines. The latter faded but the genus homo thrived. Putting
together "Homo" history is like guessing the fine detail of a dining-
room-table size jigsaw with only a cupful of pieces. Some fragments are
the remains of Homo habilis (Handy man) because they were found near
tools. Homo erectus walked tall, had a bigger brain, and more complex
tools. Homo sapiens are said to have evolved from "erectus" about
90,000 years ago, but there is little agreement after that. Looking at the
remaining fragments in our cup of pieces is rather like reading the tea
leaves. This is a slightly naughty analogy, but only slightly.

Inerrancy. The belief that Scripture does not deviate from the
truth. Biblical writers penned the words from their experience, per-
sonality, and literary talents but always under the true inspiration of
God's Spirit.

Intelligent Design. Science and theology enjoy a fruitful debate
about how we explain the incredible complexity of our world and the
universe. The scientific theologians confidently identify signs of intelli-
gence behind the complexity and even want it taught in schools and universities. Nontheological scientists argue either for pure chance or for
necessity. See Chance above.

Intermediate links were Darwin's nightmare. Why, if evolution
happened, was there no evidence of the millions of intermediate links
between various forms of life? If organic evolution was before a court of
law, the jury would want evidence of how a reptile became a bird, or a
fish turned into an amphibian, or how primitive plants turned into modern plants. Darwin thought the links would turn up one day. They
haven't, despite millions of "digs." See also Molecular biology below.

Irreducible complexity. See Intelligent Design above.

Isochron. See note 4, chapter 5.

Lamina. The thinnest layer of sedimentary rock.

Laurasia. See Continental drift above.

Macro-/micro-evolution. Macro-evolution describes changes
across species, from one form of life to another. Micro-evolution is variation within a species (e.g., beaks in birds, or the differences between a
sausage dog and a St. Bernard).

Mesozoic (middle life) era from 250 to 65 million years ago.

Miocene. When human-like apes were said to appear about 25 million years ago.

Micro-evolution. See "Macro-" above.

Missing links. See Intermediate links above.

Molecular biology. Atoms are the ingredients in the recipe of molecules. Take one atom of oxygen and two of hydrogen and you have one molecule of water. The atoms run into millions in more complex molecules, such as nucleic acids. It was hoped that this, the most basic level of life, might finally hint at the missing links between the various classes of life. They don't, according to Michael Denton. "Each member of a class seems equally representative of that class, and no species appear to be in any real sense 'intermediate' between two classes," (*Evolution: A Theory in Crisis*, back cover).

Mutations are mistakes that happen in the process of reading and translating DNA. The errors are very rare and nearly always produce the weakest. Changed genes in fruit flies can make them develop an extra pair of wings or a leg where an antenna should be. A mistake of one amino acid is the difference between normal hemoglobin and sickle-cell hemoglobin. These mutations can be passed on to following generations. This, together with natural selection, is the driving force of evolution, say evolutionists. Creationist science argues that the vast number of mutations are either sterile or backward steps, or prove fatal to their host.

Natural selection is the posh name for "survival of the fittest." Wherever there is competition for food or in harsh environments, those fittest will always survive to breed, and therefore the species can be changed by increasing levels of adaptation.

Neanderthal man is said by evolutionists to be chinless, large faced, heavy browed, and with a low, sloping head. They became extinct. Creationists believe they were a degenerative and diseased variety of Homo sapiens.

Necessity. See Chance and Intelligent Design above.

Oligocene. Our pets developed in this age (part of Tertiary) 65–25 million years ago.

Ordovician. The ancient tribe of Ordovices inhabited the Arenig Mountains of North Wales, and when a significant stratum containing distinctive graptolite fossils was found there, it earned the tribal name. The era ran from 500 to 430 million years ago.

Pangaea. See Continental drift above.

Permian. Pangaea developed in this period (280–225 million years ago).

Phanerozoic. Obvious life.

Plate tectonics is the idea that the outer shell of the earth is divided into seven large plates and many smaller ones that move about in relation to one another. Matching coastlines across oceans and seafloor spreading support the theory. See Continental drift above.

Precambrian covers the supposed massive epoch between the

earth's formation to about 570 million years ago. A few simple life forms have been found at this level, plus worm-like trail marks. Some of the oldest rocks are found at Isua in East Greenland.

Punctuated equilibria is an alternative way of describing the progress of evolution. Charles Darwin insisted that change could only come about by slow, gradual processes. Paleontologists, like the late Stephen Jay Gould and Niles Eldredge, argued that the fossil record did not show this. They proposed that species were stable (in equilibria) for long periods but these were punctuated by short bursts of sudden change. Many modern evolutionists have grown up with this idea and accept it.

Pyroclastic flow. Fragments thrown out by volcanic eruption and flowing with gas away from a vent.

Quaternary is the most recent era of life, from 2.5 million years ago to present day.

Radiometric dating is taken from various "earth clocks." The age of rocks can be gauged by the rate of decay of various elements within them. Elements like argon and uranium decay into daughter elements. Each has a half-life. Creationists claim that these clocks are not reliable because of unknown variables, as outlined in chapter 5.

Red Shift. See Doppler effect above.

RNA. See DNA above.

Rodinia. See Continental drift above.

Second Law of Thermodynamics. See Entropy above.

Silurian. The ancient Welsh tribe of the Silures lives on, their name being borrowed to describe a short era from 430 to 390 million years ago.

Steady State theory argues that the universe will always look like it is today, because its expansion is always being matched by the creation of new matter that condenses into new galaxies. Background radiation, the alleged "noise" of the Big Bang, plus other cosmic evidence, indicates that Fred Hoyle's Steady State theory is shaky. One of the amazing phenomena of our incredible universe is how cosmologists can stake their lives and reputations on theories of a universe we know next to nothing about.

Survival of the fittest. See Natural selection above.

Theistic evolutionists believe that God *(theos)* is the driving force of evolution and that early Genesis is a nonliteral picture of creation.

Thixotropic. Look carefully at very old windows and the glass will be thicker at the bottom. Thixotrophy is the fluid property of material like glass. Even when cold and solid, it moves. When heated or under abnormal stress, glass and plastic can, of course, return to more fluid states. A layer of material on which the earth's tectonic plates are thought to rest is said to be governed by this property, and was responsible for one super continent breaking up over millions of years to form the present land masses.

Transitional links. See Intermediate links above.

Triassic. The 30-million-year age of the minidinosaurs around 300 million years ago.

Trilobites were named after the three lobes that ran the length of their outer shells. They ranged in length from a few millimeters to 65cm (26 inches). They are said to have evolved rapidly with a world-wide tenancy and were therefore used to date the rocks in which they were found. In some instances, the trilobites were dated by the rock they were found in. This sounds like double-dutch circular reasoning. It is one of the problems in dating (see chapter 6).

Uniformitarianism. See Catastrophism above.

INDEX

❖ READERS' GUIDE

**FOR PERSONAL REFLECTION
OR GROUP DISCUSSION**

Introduction to the Readers' Guide

As you began reading *Responding to the Challenge of Evolution*, you probably already understood that you could hardly have undertaken to read about a more complicated subject. But don't be alarmed! We think that this book will take you to new levels of thought and provide you with information you will be grateful for.

There will probably be two types of readers for this book: People for whom this will be a challenge, and those who will enjoy the romp and move on to something more complex. There is no doubt that this book barely scratches the surface of the evolution versus creation issue, but it should also serve the purpose of getting the reader to do some deeper thinking—either to dig deeper or to work to understand this information more clearly.

Because this book starts off by recording a situation of conflict about teaching creationism in the school system, we hope you will also have a desire to understand what you and the children are being taught as factual regarding this subject. Consequently, some of the

exercises we ask you to work through are designed to see if this subject could actually be taught side by side with evolution. Would it
create confusion? Are the two approaches so strongly opposed to
each other that this would be impossible? We also hope you will
embrace the truths you learn, however much they may conflict with
what you have been "taught" through school, news, and other media.

We hope you were shocked by the knowledge that other countries
are embracing and teaching their children about creationism. Perhaps
this book will challenge you to begin to teach creationism to your
children yourself or to push for it in your child's school system. If so,
please don't shy away from it; for the best way to learn is to teach!

Ultimately, we believe that you will grow through the study questions regardless of your level of understanding of this subject. We
would rather see you drawn to God as Creator than to try to force this
belief onto you, and we believe the study guide will allow you to
come to conclusions that will ultimately lead you to him.

Enjoy your journey, and may God richly bless you with understanding along the way.

READERS' GUIDE QUESTIONS:

CHAPTER 1

1. The author states that he is merely a reporter of facts, theories, and expert opinion. Is this a role you would model to non-believers or Christians who believe in evolution? Why or why not?

2. As a Christian, do you personally believe in creation or evolution? Has that always been your belief, or does this represent a change for you? Defend your position.

3. Regarding *On the Origin of Species*, the book that began this debate, do you understand the proposals therein? Do you think it's important to understand Darwin's work in order to defend your choice? Explain why.

CHAPTER 2

1. If 47 percent of Americans and many scientists believe we were created by God, what do you think the debate about teaching creationism in the schools and reporting it in scientific journals is about?

2. If creationism is taught in so many other countries—countries not typically known as Christ-centered—and we do not teach it in America, what does that say about the direction of this nation? Does that concern you? Why?

3. Discuss any surprises you found in the various categories of creationism in this chapter. Did the categories help you define or further confuse your own "category"?

4. The author states that Star Trek is responsible for some aspects of the reverent agnostic's belief and thought process. Explain how you feel about that. Can contemplating Star Trek truly lead one to understand truth?

CHAPTER 3

1. As you contemplate the actual age of the earth and the methods people have used to date it, are you inclined to want to change your "category" of creationism? Do the newer dating methods seem more reliable or less reliable to you? How does your level of confidence in scientific methods affect your ability to defend your position?

2. Are you more inclined toward faith as your answer to the profound question of the age of the earth, or are you being drawn more into science to define your answer? Explain.

3. Has your idea of the earth's age been simplified or complicated by these methods of measurements?

4. Did you switch from being an Old Earther to a Young Earther through this information, or vice-versa? Has the info shored up your beliefs or challenged them?

CHAPTER 4

1. After learning some of the complexities of measuring the earth's age, are you conflicted now about the simplicity of the Young Earthers' position? Explain.

2. If you are a novice in this area, what are your thoughts as you consider such things as catastrophic events and salty seas? Up to now, have your opinions been based on fact or faith, and is that shifting?

3. If you have studied these issues before, how have the facts and opinions of Young Earthers affected your own opinions and your ability to discuss them with either evolutionists or creationists?

4. How has your personal belief system survived this information so far? Are you on more solid ground than before, or are you beginning to understand how one might choose a side and stick to it just to have the matter decided?

CHAPTER 5

1. The author states that there are two schools of thought on dating the earth. One is that dating must be accurate or the whole thing falls apart, and the other is that dating can't be accurate because past atmospheric conditions can't be known. Do you think that dating is that important, and do you think there is or can be an accurate method of dating? Defend your opinion.

2. Both sides of the dating argument appear to have at least some solid proof their theory is correct. Can it be argued that either side has all the facts? Discuss what you think seems most reasonable, and why.

CHAPTER 6

1. The author asserts that it is "circular thinking" to state that strata can be dated by the fossils they contain, and the fossils themselves can be dated by the strata they are found in. Based on the number of dating methods available, is this a good system to use? Why or why not?

2. If the circular thinking theory gave rise to the geological column and circular thinking is incorrect, can the geological column be correct?

3. Could—as Old Earthers assert—something as random as evolution have occurred uniformly around the earth? What case can be made for supporting this theory?

CHAPTER 7

1. What do the "ologists" stand to lose by questioning their own theories? What do they stand to gain?

2. Provide your own examples of micro-evolution, or provide your evidence that it doesn't exit.

3. Does the fact that humans can selectively breed animals for certain characteristics lead you to believe that they are creating new species? Discuss the differences, if any, between adaptation and variation.

Chapter 8

1. Based on the availability of rapid, extensive world travel and the quality and quantity of scientific equipment and methods we have at our disposal today, could Darwin have developed his theory today?

2. If your answer to the question above was no, discuss why so many people cling to Darwin's theory today.

3. Based on the information in this chapter, which do you think came first: the belief in evolution or the proof of evolution? Defend your position.

4. Within the community of evolutionists exists confusion and conflict, as it does in the creationists' camp. Discuss why you think this occurs and why, in spite of it, evolutionism has outstripped creationism.

Chapter 9

1. The book *The Genesis Flood* enabled creationists to understand the impact of the flood upon the scientific community and gained

much acceptance in the world. What is your theory of why we are no more widely accepted now than we were then?

2. Natural selection seems to be a subjective theory. Do you feel this subjectivity weakens the theory or causes one to doubt the scientist? Why?

3. In reading about the many irreducible complexities in the body, what seems to be the obvious conclusion? Why do scientists prefer to say that there can never be a conclusion to explain these complexities? Why do you think more scientific information is providing fewer answers to these scientists?

CHAPTER 10

1. Darwin is considered a courageous man for stating his claims to the world. How do current evolutionists measure up to Darwin's example? Considering how they are presenting their information, would you consider today's scientists courageous?

2. As scientists debate the fossil record, what are your thoughts regarding the subject? Explain how the status of the fossil record proves or disproves Darwin.

3. Considering Darwin's courage in stating his findings, what do you think he would write today with the information available to him? Do you think he would be able to hold to his original theory?

CHAPTER 11

1. The strongest piece of the puzzle Steve Jones has is, seemingly, what isn't there. How is this lack of information affecting your own interpretation of the theory of evolution?

2. Evolutionists are trying to prove a beginning of the human race through the ape; creationists believe that there was a man and a woman in a garden—placed there by God. What do you suppose draws evolution scientists to such an obscure theory, especially when so little of their "evidence" holds up over time?

3. Scientists are racing to prove that they have found skeletons that will prove their theories. What are your thoughts pertaining to this? What kind of evidence would have to be discovered to convince you that the missing link truly had been found?

4. What were your thoughts when you first heard of the so-called "missing links" when you were in school? Was this information presented to you as fact or as historical hoax?

CHAPTER 12

1. You've read some incredible examples of tiny life forms and the intricacies of what they do to survive. The author asks the question, "Design or Chance?" What do you think, and why?

2. What impressed you the most about what you read? Is it significant enough that you would like this information available in the

schools? Would you teach it in your own home? Would you want to discuss the information in a class in your Sunday school?

3. Let us ask you to take a challenge now. Choose one of the examples in this chapter, and if you are a creationist, take an honest attempt at explaining your example through evolution. If you are an evolutionist, explain it as creationist belief.

4. Did this experiment convince you of the opposite point of view? Has it made you more understanding of the opposing point of view? Were you able to be convincing in any way as you attempted this challenge?

5. Would this experiment be beneficial during a conversation with a person of the opposite belief?

Chapter 13

1. What are your thoughts on Polkinghorne's statement: "I do not believe that God directly wills either the act of a murderer, or the incidence of a cancer. I believe he allows both to happen in a creation to which he has given the gift of being itself." Does this fit with your belief system?

2. Rewrite Polkinghorne's statement to reflect your own understanding of the relationship between free will and chance.

CHAPTER 14

1. As the author explained in this chapter, sometimes—in spite of all scientific facts, Scriptures, discoveries—one still has a gut feeling about this subject. Most likely that's true with you. But have you changed at all during the course of this study, or are you more convinced than ever—in your gut—that you're right?

2. If you haven't changed your mind in any way, have you found any information that had an impact on you? What was it, and to what extent were you influenced?

CHAPTER 15

1. Imagine yourself in the position of having been alive during the first century of civilization. You know nothing of science, but you are familiar with God. What would be your understanding of Genesis 1?

2. What would God be telling you through this text?

3. In that early setting, what would you think of someone who would challenge your understanding of the world, as Darwin did to a civilization that knew some, but very little of science.

4. Do you now view yourself as being sure of what you know, and confident that science backs up your belief, or have you come to realize that much of the subject isn't worth alienating the lost by being adamant that you're right?

CHAPTER 16

1. The author states that the Gap Theory is now out of favor, but that it was once quite popular. Are you familiar with this theory? When or how did you first hear of it?

2. Does the Gap Theory answer any issues for you, or are you uncomfortable with it? Explain your thoughts.

3. What do you think of people who might still choose to believe this theory?

4. Which "day theory" do you think describes your own philosophy? Why?

CHAPTER 17

1. Do you believe the creationists' claim that the church itself is responsible for the Scriptures being held in such low regard? Do you believe that the situation can be reversed? How?

2. Do you think the fact that some portions of the creation story simply can't be proved with scientific methods is a weakness in the creation argument? What, if anything, could overcome that?

3. What do you think could be the reason(s) God allowed so many accounts of the Genesis story to be recorded as fact throughout the Bible?

4. As you read the fifteen-billion-year timeline, which parts were easy for you to believe? Which parts were difficult or impossible for you to believe? Discuss why.

5. Can a case be made that the strong communication skills of God and his essential goodness are a predictor of the reliability of Scriptures?

6. Does it necessarily follow that everything contradictory to Scripture comes from Satan? Why or why not?

CHAPTER 18

1. Do you think all the evidence cited by evolutionists would be able to stand if scientists were open to honest challenges from colleagues? Would a free exchange of ideas lead to a better understanding of the world, or would it have little impact on the way we see our universe?

2. Can any human—whether scientist or layperson—ever be truly objective when faith conflicts with science? Does this have any bearing on our ability to persuade others of the validity of our position? Why or why not?

3. If it is true that only God's Spirit can reveal truth to our hearts, do you think Christians need to keep abreast of current issues?

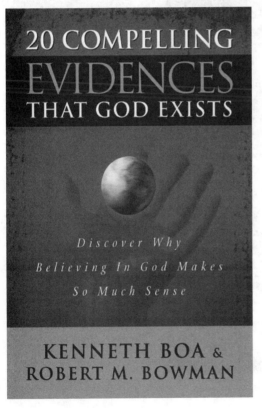

You're a new Christian—now what? This bestselling book helps believers understand the central truths of Christianity.

0-78143-964-7
Item # 102857
5 1/2 X 8 1/2 • Paperback • 208 p

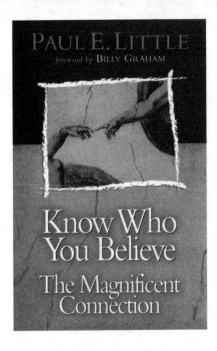
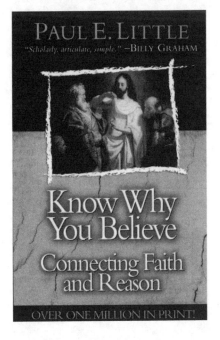

Additional copies of *RESPONDING TO THE CHALLENGES OF EVOLUTION* and other Victor titles are available from your local bookseller.

If you have enjoyed this book,
or if it has had an impact on your life,
we would like to hear from you.

Please contact us at:

VICTOR BOOKS
Cook Communications Ministries, Dept. 201
4050 Lee Vance View
Colorado Springs, CO 80918
Or visit our Web site: www.cookministries.com

For our European readers:
KINGSWAY COMMUNICATIONS LTD
Lottbridge Drove, Eastbourne BN23 6NT, England
E-mail: books@kingsway.co.uk

Victor®
The Bible Teacher's Teacher

The Word at Work Around the World

A vital part of Cook Communications Ministries is our international outreach, Cook Communications Ministries International (CCMI). Your purchase of this book, and of other books and Christian-growth products from Cook, enables CCMI to provide Bibles and Christian literature to people in more than 150 languages in 65 countries.

Cook Communications Ministries is a not-for-profit, self-supporting organization. Revenues from sales of our books, Bible curricula, and other church and home products not only fund our U.S. ministry, but also fund our CCMI ministry around the world. One hundred percent of donations to CCMI go to our international literature programs.

CCMI reaches out internationally in three ways:

· Our premier International Christian Publishing Institute (ICPI) trains leaders from nationally led publishing houses around the world.

· We provide literature for pastors, evangelists, and Christian workers in their national language.

· We reach people at risk—refugees, AIDS victims, street children, and famine victims—with God's Word.

Word Power, God's Power

Faith Kidz, RiverOak, Honor, Life Journey, Victor, NexGen — every time you purchase a book produced by Cook Communications Ministries, you not only meet a vital personal need in your life or in the life of someone you love, but you're also a part of ministering to José in Colombia, Humberto in Chile, Gousa in India, or Lidiane in Brazil. You help make it possible for a pastor in China, a child in Peru, or a mother in West Africa to enjoy a life-changing book. And because you helped, children and adults around the world are learning God's Word and walking in his ways.

Thank you for your partnership in helping to disciple the world. May God bless you with the power of his Word in your life.

For more information about our international ministries, visit www.ccmi.org.